Iakwbou

Terry Kwanghyun Eum

CreateSpace
North Charleston, SC

Iakwbou
ISBN-10: 1508476055
ISBN-13: 978-1508476054

For

ἡ βασιλεία τοῦ θεου

My Father, 음동명

My Mother,이충옥

My Beloved Wife, Chelsea I. Eum

My Father-In-Law, Charles E. Lange

My Mother-In-Law, Cathy A. Lange

My Brother-In-Law, Chad E. Lange

My Beloved Friend, 신재석

My Best Friend, 김민욱

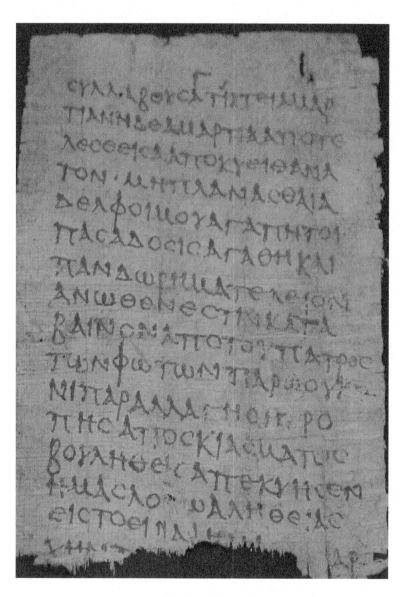

Papyrus 23 (Gregory-Aland)
Fragment of the Book of James

Acknowledgement

This commentary has grown out of my teaching of the Book of James. My beloved congregants of the Living Grace Ministry at Emmaus United Methodist Church at Stratford Hills have been my primary conversation partners, and I am thankful for the privilege of engaging biblical texts with such faithful, intelligent, and interesting people of God.

After finished writing a commentary, *"Kata Markon"* I was searching for some other books from the New Testament to study, meditate, teach and write. Thus I started asking some of my *"inner-circle"* a question: *"What is your favorite book from the New Testament besides the Gospels?"* My Mother-In-Law told me that she was reading the Book of James, while she was pregnant with my wife, Chelsea. She was reading the Book of James even when she was in hospital in January 15th of 1985, a week before my wife was born. Then I also learned that my Brother-In-Law's favorite book from the Bible was the Book of James as well.

As I publish this commentary, I'd like to publically express my love and gratitude to my beloved wife, Chelsea I. Eum who raises our three gifts from God Isaac, Caleb, and Enoch lovingly, and beautifully.

Also I express my love and appreciation to my father-in-laws, Charles E. Lange, mother-in-law, Cathy A. Lange, and my brother-in-law, Chad A. Lange whom showed hospitality, the love of the Lord, and faith through their lives.

평생 당신들의 삶으로 아들에게 하나님의 사랑, 신앙을 보여주시고, 기도해 주신, 교육하신, 하나님의 신앙의 용장들, 아버지, 음동명 장로님, 어머니, 이충옥 권사님께 이 책을 출판하며 사랑과 감사 전합니다.

또한 인생에서 중요한 두 친구에게도 감사표시를 합니다. 저자의 성장, 발전, 변화를 대화와 삶으로 수용해주고 떨어져서도 늘 함께 해준, "*Best Friend*"이자 "형"인 김민욱 형, Michigan 에서 한 교회의 성장과 발전을, 신앙과 교회의 문화를 위해 고민하시는, "*테리야, 행동 없는 믿음은 가짜 믿음이야!*" 하시는 신재석 집사님께 감사의 인사를 전합니다.

Through my research of the Book of James, I discerned that it is a very important book for the life of the Christian Community. May this commentary enlighten you what our God through the Book of James, "*Iakwbou*" is trying to tell you.

Terry Kwanghyun Eum
Richmond, Virginia

Contents

Excursuses

Introduction

The Book/Letter of James is one of the more useful and practical books in the New Testament. However, it has never been a very popular book, thanks in large part to Martin Luther, the great Protestant reformer, who disparaged James as an *"epistle of straw."* Luther's comments are the best known criticisms of the book, and the stigma of his condemnation haunts it to this day.

Still, if Luther and others have been less than enthusiastic about James, the reasons are readily apparent. Upon first reading the letter, one is struck by the glaring absence of central tenets of Christian faith. In particular, one looks in vain for any reference to the life and ministry of Jesus, or to his death and resurrection. There are, in fact, only two brief references to Jesus in the whole book, which can be found in verses 1:1 and 2:1. James has more to say about Rahab the prostitute than about Jesus!

Moreover, the book is short on grace and long on *"works"* and thus has had the misfortune of appearing to contradict the New Testament's preeminent apostle, Paul, who maintained that we are saved by grace through faith apart from works of the law (Rom. 3:28). For all of these reasons, Luther complained that James has "nothing of the nature of the gospel about it" and denounced it as an *"epistle of straw."*

At first glance, James is a peculiar book. Misgivings about it are laid to rest, however, when one important fact about the nature of James is understood: James' letter is what interpreters refer to as *paraenesis*, or ethical exhortation, in the form of a letter. *"Paraenesis"* is derived from the Greek word *"parainesis,"* which means *"advice"* or *"counsel"* or *"exhortation."* Paraenesis is ethical exhortation, that is, instruction concerning how one ought to live. This insight is crucial for one's reading and interpretation of this book, for the purpose of the book then becomes clear: James is not trying to evangelize the world; instead, it is calling its readers to live the Christian life.

The Book of James is not a missionary document; it is an in-house document, a document for use within the church. Thus it should come as no surprise that James does not present the whole of Christian truth, for it is addressed to readers who have already heard the gospel and embraced it and who are very familiar with the central tenets of Christian faith. What we hear in James is the voice not of a preacher but of a teacher, one who is anxious to help believers see the implications of Christian faith for behavior – for how they live out their lives. This is the focus of James. James urges believers to apply Christian faith to every aspect of life.

James is not the only point at which one finds paraenesis or ethical exhortation in the New Testament. Paul's letters, for example, usually conclude with short paraenetical sections (cf. 1 Thess. 4-5, Gal. 5-6, Rom. 12-14), in which Paul provides very direct advice as to how people who have embraced the gospel should live. James, however, uses paraensis throughout – from beginning to end. As biblical commentator Sophie Law observes, the Book of James is *"the most consistently ethical document in the New Testament."* It is one of the New Testament's most persistent reminders that genuine Christian faith has implications for how we live our lives.

Indeed, James has been referred to as a *"showcase of Christian living,"* and no aspect of our lives is too small to be placed on exhibit. The book lifts up a remarkable variety of practical concerns, and readers will find that it is extraordinarily relevant and concrete. For example, have you ever put your foot in your mouth? Have you ever been tormented by the memory of words you with you have never said? James has much to say about the awesome power of our tongues to heal and to hurt and about the importance of disciplined speech.

In five short chapters, the Book of James discerns (among other things) the relevance of Christian faith to our speech, to our economic pursuits and business practices, to our experiences of trial and temptation, to our responses to discrimination and to people in need, and to our life together in the Christian community. James deals almost exclusively with the social and practical aspects of Christianity. It reminds us of the everyday problems with which we struggle and maintains that Christian faith touches every aspect of life, transforming routine pursuits into opportunities for discipleship.

By the time we reach James in the New Testament, we have already heard the gospel. We are already familiar with the central tenets of Christian faith. But believers do not live by theology alone. What do we do? How do we live? What are the implications of Christian faith for how we live our lives? These are questions that confront us daily and this is where James helps us out. This is the point at which James is one of the more useful and practical books in the New Testament. It is, indeed, a showcase of Christian living, and behind every exhibit, and implicit in every line, is the central theme of this book: the wholeness and integrity of Christian life. To see that theme embodied in the life of the church is the book's primary goal as well. James' hope, expressed in the opening verses of the book, is that we may be *"mature and complete, lacking in nothing"* (1:4).

The Book/Letter of James challenges us to be people of integrity, that is, people who are consistent in all we see, say, believe, and do. Throughout the letter, by way of negative example, the author draws our attention to the *"double-minded person"* (cf. 1:8; 4:8) – the person beset by double-vision, double-talk, and double-face – and expresses a hope that we, by contrast, will manifest integrity of faith. From the first verse to the last, James calls us to behavior consistent with our convictions and inspires us to live our faith.

In this commentary, I will use the New International Version (NIV) Bible translation as well as my raw translation (Terry's Translation, "*TT*") of each text from the biblical Greek.

James as Wisdom Writing

The address *"to the twelve tribes in the Diaspora"* (1:1), probably referring to scattered Jewish-Christian congregations (it is the reason why the book is included among the general or catholic Epistles), however, it echoes the later Jewish Wisdom literature.

As Moral exhortation (There are some 59 imperatives in its 108 verses), James can be compared to other ancient writings whose concern is the practical wisdom of right behavior. James resembles the popular moral philosophy of the Greco-Roman world in its insistence on control of the passions and of speech and on the demonstration of verbal profession in practice, as well as in its perception of envy and arrogance as destructive vices. The specific symbolic world of James, however, is that of Torah. James appropriates the multiple dimensions of Torah in a way distinctive among New Testament writings. First, James has a positive view of the *"law,"* not as a set of ritual obligations but as moral commandment expressed most perfectly by what it calls *"the law of the kingdom"* or *"royal law"* – namely, the law of love of neighbor from Lev. 19:18 (James 2:8-13). Second, James appropriates the voice of the prophets in its understanding of human life as fundamentally covenantal and relational and in its harsh condemnation of those whose desire for self-aggrandizement leads them to oppress and defraud others (4:13-5:6). Third, James represents the Wisdom tradition of Torah, not only in its liberal use of proverb and maxim, but also by understanding human freedom in terms of an allegiance either to a *"wisdom from above"* or to a *"wisdom from below"* (1:5; 3:13-18).

As a kind of wisdom literature, James naturally bears a certain resemblance to the wide range of wisdom writings that were produced in the ancient Near East. Wisdom has an international character, not only because human behavior does show some constants across cultures, but also because wisdom literature was produced by scribes in ancient bureaucracies who borrowed freely from other cultures in shaping wisdom for their own. Torah within the wider cultural setting of Hellenism, such as the *Sentences of Pseudo-Phocylides* and the *Testaments of the Twelve Patriarchs*. When a thorough comparison is made between James and all these other wisdom writings, however, the distinctiveness of James emerges more clearly.

There are four ways in which James stands out among all ancient moral literature. First, James' concern is with morals rather than manners. Much of the moral exhortation of antiquity dealt with finding and keeping one's place in the world as a means to success and honor. James has none of those concerns, but deals exclusively with moral attitudes and behavior. Second, James addresses an intentional community rather than a household. It has nothing about obligations within the household or the state, nothing about duties owed by parents to children or

slaves to masters. It says nothing about sexual morality.
Its attention is exclusively devoted to an *"ecclesia"* (church,
faith community, gathering, assembly) gathered by
common values and convictions, summarized by faith in
Jesus Christ (2:1). Third, James is egalitarian rather than
hierarchical. Much of ancient wisdom assumes and
reinforces the differences in status, especially between
parents and children. In James, the only kinship language
is that of *"brother and sister,"* with even the author
presenting himself as a *"slave"* (1:1) rather than as an
authority. God is the only "father" in this community
(1:17-18, 27). The egalitarian outlook of James is shown as
well in its condemnation of favoritism in judging (2:1, 9)
and every form of boasting (3:14-15) and arrogance (4:6),
slander and judging (4:11-12). Fourth, James is
communitarian rather than individualistic. Against every
form of self-assertion that seeks advantage at the expense
of another, James calls for attitudes of solidarity, mercy,
and compassion. In contrast to the logic of envy that leads
to oppression and *"killing the righteous one"* (5:6), James
calls for a community that rallies around the sick and sinful
in order to heal/save them (5:14-16).

Authorship

Who is the author who speaks to us through this challenging letter? We don't know! In the opening verse of the letter, the author is identified simply as *"James, a slave of God and of the Lord Jesus Christ"* (1:1). *"James"* is one of the most common of Jewish and Christian names. Indeed, there are five individuals named *"James,"* mentioned elsewhere in the New Testament, who are likely candidates:

1. James, the son of Zebedee (Mark 1:19; 3:17; Acts 12:2)

2. James, the father of Jude (Luke 6:16; Acts 1:13)

3. James, the son of Alphaeus (Mark 3:18)

4. James the younger (Mark 15:40)

5. James the brother of Jesus (Mark 6:3; 1 Cor. 15:7; Gal. 1:19; 2:9, 12; Acts 12:17; 15:13; 21:18; Jude 1)

Church tradition has attributed the letter to the final and best-known candidate: James the brother of the Lord and the leader of the early Christian community in Jerusalem. However, the author nowhere identifies himself as a leader of the church nor as a relative of Jesus. Did James of Jerusalem in fact write this letter?

Some interpreters maintain that he did, since what is known of James of Jerusalem is consistent with the character of the letter. According to historians, this James was a dedicated advocate of Jewish-Christian piety who attached great importance to observance of the Jewish law. Since he was martyred in 62 C.E., his authorship would make the Book of James one of the earliest writings of the New Testament.

Many interpreters, however, are not persuaded that James of Jerusalem wrote the letter. Indeed, a number of factors argue against it:

1. The letter is written in relatively polished and literary Greek. There is some question as to whether the cultured language of the letter would have been in the command of James of Jerusalem, an Aramaic-speaking Palestinian Jew.

2. Nowhere does the author indicate that he is the Lord's brother or that he knew Jesus personally. One wonders why a Christian with such a special relationship with the Lord would make such scant reference to him.

3. The discussion of "*faith*" and "*works*" in 2:14-26 seems to presuppose Paul's theological activity. In fact, as we will see, James' discussion seems to stand at some distance from the resolution of Paul's struggle with this issue in the mid-50s of the first century and to be a response to a popular misunderstanding of Paul's position.

4. One of the most serious objections to James of Jerusalem's authorship concerns the letter's view of the law.

James of Jerusalem's well known devotion to the Jewish law placed great importance on cultic ritual matters, such as circumcision, Sabbath observance, table fellowship, and purification laws (Acts 15:13-21; 21:18-24; Gal. 2:12) – matters that are never mentioned in the Book of James. The letter's own appeal to the law or Torah, is limited to the Ten Commandments and the *"law of love"* (Lev. 19:18). In other words, when the letter of James speaks of the law, it refers not to cultic-ritual observations but to the moral teachings of the Torah.

5. Finally, it was only slowly and in the face of opposition that the Book of James came to be included in the Christian canon in the earliest centuries of the church. Its late acceptance as one of the New Testament scriptures was due to doubts about its apostolic authorship. Thus, early on, the letter does not appear to have been universally regarded as the word of the Lord's brother.

For all of these reasons, a majority of interpreters think that the author is writing under a pseudonym or alias, that is, writing in the name of someone else. In this case he is using the name of James, the revered leader of the Jerusalem church, and associating his teaching with James' tradition and authority. It is important to remind ourselves that there were no shady connotations associated with this practice! We cannot impose our modern notions of intellectual property and copyright laws on first-century writings. Writing under a pseudonym was a common, acceptable practice in ancient times. It was a way of honoring that person and claiming to stand in the same tradition.

Thus while it is impossible to date the letter with any certainty, it is generally thought to have been written toward the end of the first century, well after Paul's activity in the mid-50s and after the death of James of Jerusalem in 62 C.E. – at a time when the martyred James of Jerusalem had become a revered figure of the past.

Whatever the case may be, we know for certain that the author was a teacher. James 3:1 provides our only clue: *"Not many of you should become teachers, my brothers and sisters, for you know that we who teach will be judged with greater strictness."* The author is an early Christian teacher, one who was responsible for guiding the early Christian community in many aspects of its life. In fact, the Book of James may serve as an example of the work of early Christian teachers (Eph. 4:11-13).

However, in the opening verse of the letter, the author refers to himself simply and humbly as a *"slave,"* thereby giving expression only to his commitment, obedience, and loyalty to the God who has been made known in Jesus Christ. His specific identity will probably continue to be a matter of debate, and there is room for disagreement in this matter. But fortunately, while his identity is shrouded in mystery, one thing – the most important thing – is quite clear: his message for us today!

Theology

James is one of the most theologically (as distinct from Christologically) dense and robust writings in the New Testament. James presents God as one, the very model of integrity (2:19). God is the Creator, the unchanging *"Father of lights"* (1:17), the giver of every good gift. God does not struggle with evil and is not the source of the evil against which the righteous struggle (1:13); rather evil takes root in self-centered human desires. God's will is to give birth to a new creation through the word of truth (1:18). God is the generous source of wisdom from above (1:5; 3:17) who gives to those who pray with undivided minds. God is the Lawgiver and Judge (4:12; 2:11), whose law liberates us from enslavement to selfish ambition to lives of loving service (2:12). Yet despite our failings in many ways (3:2), God is merciful and gracious to the humble (4:6); God is ready to be found by those who seek God with their whole hearts (4:7-10). God shows special concern for the poor, choosing them to be rich within the sphere of faith and heirs of the kingdom of God (2:5; 1:9; 4:6). God rewards those who stand firm in the struggle out of love for God (1:12). God befriends those who, as Abraham did, share God's active concern for those in need (2:23); such active, compassionate religion meets God's approval (1:27). Yet, for those who practice injustice and exploitation, God is Lord Almighty (5:4), who heeds the cries of the oppressed and comes speedily to their aid. God works for justice but does so apart from human anger (1:20; 3:18). God spoke through the prophets who challenged the injustices of their days "*in the name of the Lord*" (5:10). Job serves as an example of one who persevered and discovered God brought his story to a merciful and compassionate end (5:11). In a shrinking world in which inter-faith dialogue among adherents of the great monotheistic faiths is needed, James serves as a witness to common roots and shared convictions of those who serve one God.

Christology

S. Laws contended James *"has no apparent interest in Jesus as a redeemer-figure."* Rather James views Jesus as a teacher, *"present Lord whose authority is acknowledge in daily life,"* and *"future judge."* For James, Christianity consists in fulfilling the commandments and instructions of the Lord, who will be the final Judge. Within the larger New Testament context, James functions as the probing question *"Why do you call me 'Lord, Lord,' and do not do what I tell you?"* (Luke 6:46). That is, James is a warning against a Christianity that neglects the role of Jesus as Teacher and empties the term Lord of its meaning as one whose authority is acknowledged in daily life. Others have noted similar Christological emphases in Q, the Sermon on the Mount, and other literature. Although James does not explicitly refer to Jesus as Teacher or identify traditional material as Jesus' teachings, James may view the *"royal law"* of neighbor love (2:8) as kingly because Jesus singled it out and because it epitomizes the ethics of the kingdom Jesus preached.

Soteriology

Does salvation for James indeed consist in fulfilling the commandments and instructions of the Lord? James answers, *"In fulfillment of his own purpose he gave us birth by the word of truth, so that we would become a kind of firstfruits of his creatures"* (1:18). Assuming these images of (re)generation and firstfruits refer to salvation, the question remains: To what does the word of truth refer? This word is identical with *"the implanted word that has the power to save your souls"* (1:21). This word is one that must be welcomed, i.e., heard and practiced with meekness (1:21). Since the call to be doers of the word follows immediately upon this call to welcome the word with meekness, this charge is naturally a call to put this implanted word into practice in the believer's life (1:22). Indeed, welcoming or receiving the word involves becoming a doer of the word. Likewise, the perfect law, the law of liberty (1:25) is a functional equivalent of the implanted word in that one can be a doer of both. Later, James indicates the law of liberty is a standard for judgment that pertains to right speaking and doing (2:12). At the judgment, God blesses whoever contemplates that perfect law and goes on to become a doer of that word (1:25). Similarly, the do-nothing hearer is self-deceived (1:22) and will be found wanting at judgment (2:13-14, 16).

James 5:19 warns that one can wander from the truth (and can be brought back). James does not seem to be talking about a doctrinal error but the departure from a way of life. Salvation for James is connected with restoration to this way of truth: *"Whoever brings back a sinner from [his] wandering [way] will save the sinner's soul from death"* (5:20).

The word of truth and its synonyms – the implanted word, the word, the perfect law, the law of liberty, and the truth – perhaps refers to the letter as a whole, and the tradition that stands behind it. This moral tradition with its many links to the sayings of Jesus must be received and practiced in meekness as a right way of speaking and doing, since it will be the basis for God's judgment. The letter thus prepares hearers for that judgment by clarifying the criterion. The letter models restoration of sinners to the way of truth by instruction in the heavenly wisdom that they are called to practice (3:17). If Christianity for James consists primarily in adherence to a way of life before God, *"the Way"* that Jesus taught, then the letter serves as a handbook or epitome to this body of oral teaching. Perhaps this handbook was used in the training of new converts, perhaps as part of their baptismal catechesis or instruction. Perhaps the letter served as a church manual for restoration to the Christian community.

The Recipients of the Letter

Neither can we say with certainty to whom the Book of James was first addressed. The church has regarded James as one of the "*general*," or "*catholic*" (that is, universal), epistles. These epistles are not like Paul's letters, which are addressed to specific congregations and places – to the churches in Galatia, Thessalonica, Philippi, or Rome. The general epistles, such as James, Jude, and 1 and 2 Peter, carry the name of the author rather than of the recipients, because they appear to be addressed to Christians in general rather than to a specific community at a particular place. They appear to have been written for general distribution and to address issues in the wider church. The opening verse of the Book of James, for example, greets "*the twelve tribes in the Diaspora*" (1:1). The "*twelve tribes*" is a way of referring to the Jewish nation, and Jews in the "*Diaspora*" lived outside of Palestine, scattered among the nations. "*The twelve tribes in the Diaspora*," however, is very likely a reference to all Christians as heirs of the Jewish tradition, for the early Christians viewed themselves as such and freely applied Jewish titles to themselves.

James, therefore, addresses a large audience: the whole of God's people scattered throughout the world! It speaks of general rather than particular situations.

However, the discussion that follows does relate to actual history, in that it indicates those areas of life in the early Christian community that the author found to be most urgently in need of direction and regulation.

The areas of Christian life to which James devotes attention continue to be those areas that are urgently in need of direction and regulation today. This first-century letter is startlingly relevant in our century. In fact, a word of warning is in order: James is strong medicine, which we may find hard to swallow at some points! James hits close to home, for many of the defects the author discerns in his churches are found in contemporary churches as well.

However, if we carefully attend to this letter, the Book of James could accomplish a renewing of our Christian lives. May James renew us for years to come!

(The Letter) Of James

ΙΑΚΩΒΟΥ

James 1:1 → Author and Audience

NIV	TT
1¹ James, a servant of God and of the Lord Jesus Christ, To the twelve tribes scattered among the nations: Greetings.	1¹ **James**¹, **a slave of God**² and of the Lord Jesus Christ, To the twelve tribes in the **Diaspora**³: **Greetings**⁴.

Readers must have been expected to recognize that *"James"* was the brother of the Lord. Later traditions about James consistently refer to his piety.

---

¹ Ἰάκωβος → James in Greek is *Ἰάκωβος* (Jacob), the letter is from Jacob to the twelve tribes scattered after the exile.
² θεοῦ δοῦλος → It means *"a servant of God,"* and *"a slave of God."* The phrase appears in Paul (Rom. 1:1; Gal. 1:10; Phil. 1:1), James may have taken the expression from the Old Testament (Deut. 34:5; 2 Sam. 7:5; Jer. 7:25; Amos 3:7). By adding *"and of the Lord Jesus Christ,"* James converts the older Jewish formula into a Christian designation.
³ διασπορᾷ → It means *"dispersion,"* *"Diaspora of Jews,"* and *"Diaspora of Christian."* It could refer to the geographical location of the addressees. They live outside Judea. However, the metaphorical significance of the term *"diaspora"* can indicate that the Christian community understands itself as the new gathering of the people of God that was expected in the messianic age (Jer. 3:18; Ezek. 37:19, 24; Sir. 36:13; 1QS 8:1; *2 Bar* 78:5-7). (See Excursus 2: The Diaspora)
⁴ χαίρειν → *"Greetings."* (See Excursus 1: Greetings)

- **1** The greeting follows the classic form of the Hellenistic letter. (See Excursus 1: Greetings)

Excursus 1: Greetings

Chaire was the common address on meeting people. It means *"welcome," "good day," "I am glad to see you," "good morning," "greetings"* or even *"hello."*

James employs the standard Hellenistic letter opening – Greetings (*chairein*) – in anticipation of his call to sheer joy (*charan*) in the struggle (1:2). James' *"Greetings!"* rather than the now-to-us familiar Pauline letter opening, *"Grace and peace,"* perhaps hints that James has not come to bring us peace, but to stir things up in the church!

Two positions can be adopted concerning the identification of author and recipients. If the letter was written by James, the brother of the Lord, before the year 62 C.E., then the self-designation *"slave"* of God and of the Lord Jesus Christ would suggest the confident and understated authority of a teacher (cf.3:1), and those *"in the Diaspora"* would signify Jewish Christians outside Palestine, perhaps in those regions of Antioch, Syria, and Cilicia that were clearly with Jerusalem's sphere of influence in the first generation (Acts 15:23).

Excursus 2: The Diaspora

Wherever the pioneer Christian missionaries went, they had a ready-made audience among the scattered colonies of Hellenized Jews. Their number is only an intelligent series of guesses, such as Philo made in Egypt. Perhaps 7% of the total population of the

---

21

Roman world, or some 4-4.5 million Jews, existed in the reign of Tiberius. There were about a million of them in Egypt, rather more in Syria and perhaps less than 700,000 in Palestine. There were at least 10,000 in Rome, with other large colonies in the great mercantile cities of Greece and Asia Minor. Beyond the Roman Empire, they were also massed in Mesopotamia and Media. As Josephus observed: *"There is not a community in the entire world which does not have a portion of our people."* During the struggles for power, Julius Caesar had received the support of the Jews, and his decrees on their behalf have been called their Magna Carta. For three more centuries they enjoyed special privileges, including the full freedom of worship.

If the letter is regarded as pseudonymous, then *"James"* is assumed to have been sufficiently important in the first generation for later readers to recognize his authority with no further elaboration, and *"the twelve tribes in the Diaspora"* would simply refer to all Christians, including Gentile Christians, who were far from their heavenly homeland (1 Pet. 1:1; 2:11). Whatever historical data the greeting may supply, its compositional function is to make readers of every age the recipients of a *"letter"* from the earliest days of the Christian movement and therefore, challenged by the freshness and vigor of that first generation. Christians still live in the *"Diaspora,"* they are the restored people of God, the *"twelve tribes."*

James 1:2 ~ 4 → A Perspective on Trials

NIV	TT
[2] Consider it pure joy, my brothers and sisters, whenever you face trials of many kinds, [3] because you know that the testing of your faith produces perseverance. [4] Let perseverance finish its work so that you may be mature and complete, not lacking anything.	[2] My brothers and sisters, whenever you face trials of any kind, consider it nothing but joy, [3] because you know that the testing of your faith produces endurance; [4] and let endurance have its full effect, so that you may be mature and complete, lacking in nothing.

Bad things happen to good people, and Christianity does not shelter one from the difficulties and tragedies of life. Christians share in the realities of pain, injury, loss, and sometimes oppression, which are the common lot of human experience. The author of the Book of James is keenly aware that experiences of suffering can provoke crises of faith. Thus the first thing he holds before us is a perspective with which to face the difficulties and tragedies of human life.

- **2 – 4** *"Consider it nothing but joy,"* James counsels Christian brothers and sisters, *"whenever you face trials of any kind."* The trials envisioned are not specifically identified. They are deliberately referred to as *"trials of any kind."* Whatever their nature, they are to be considered *"joy."*

  What exactly is James advising? Is it promoting a martyr complex? Are Christians actually to take pleasure in suffering? Certainly not! The various trials that we encounter – experiences of pain, loss, injury, or oppression – are not at all occasions of joy in and of themselves. Such experiences are not to be sought; nor are they to be avoided or regarded as foreign to Christian faith.

The joy of which James speaks results from the growth that trials can bring. In the midst of them, we can be drawn closer to God, experience God's sustaining power, and grow in faith and maturity. James rejoices not in trials themselves but in the steadfastness of faith and integrity of character that result from experiences of suffering. Indeed, James says not a word about why we face trials or from whence they come. The focus, instead, is on where they may lead.

James points to the joyful consequences of trial, noting first that the testing of faith produces "*endurance.*" James envisions an active steadfastness in the face of trial, not passive resignation. Passive submission to trials is not at all proposed, but rather an active, militant perseverance. In fact, Job is held up as a model of endurance in 5:11 – the Old Testament person of faith who agonizes over his predicament and struggles bitterly with his pain before friends and the LORD Almighty but who nevertheless clings tenaciously to God and refuses to yield to atheism. Such perseverance – such steadfast, heroic constancy of faith – is precisely what James views as one of the joyful consequences of trial.

Endurance, however, is not the final result of trial: *"Let endurance have its full effect, so that you may be mature and complete, lacking in nothing."* Here at the beginning of the letter is James' central theme and primary goal: the wholeness and integrity of Christian life. Trials can serve this end, for Christian life matures as the difficulties and tragedies of life are encountered, as faith *"flexes its muscles under pressure."* This is why trials can be considered *"joy"* – not because they are joyous in and of themselves but because endurance of them yields integrity and wholeness of Christian character.

James 1:5 ~ 8 → Prayer in the Midst of Trials

NIV	TT
[5] If any of you lacks wisdom, you should ask God, who gives generously to all without finding fault, and it will be given to you. [6] But when you ask, you must believe and not doubt, because the one who doubts is like a wave of the sea, blown and tossed by the wind. [7] That person should not expect to receive anything from the Lord. [8] Such a person is double-minded and unstable in all they do.	[5] If any of you is lacking in **wisdom**[5], ask God, who gives to all **generously**[6] and ungrudgingly, and it will be given you. [6] But ask in faith, never doubting, for the one who doubts is like a wave of the sea, driven and tossed by the wind; [7,8] For the doubter, being double-minded and unstable in every way, must not expect to receive anything from the Lord.

This is the theological perspective of faith that grounds a positive assessment of testing. Endurance is not the demonstration of an individual's moral character but of a community's fidelity to God as its source of being and worth. This is why the command to pray is fundamental (v.5).

---

[5] σοφία → It means "*wisdom*," "*Divine wisdom*," "*Wisdom of Christ*," and "*Wisdom of God*." Divine wisdom is a gift from God and must be sought in prayer (*Wis.* 8:21; 9:6; *Sir.* 51:13). The prayer must be full of faith and free of doubt (Mark 11:24).

[6] ἁπλῶς → It means "*without reserve*," "*generously*," and "*sincerely*." (See Excursus 3: Divine Generosity)

- **5 – 8** Divine wisdom may be needed to embrace this perspective on trials and persevere in the midst of them. It is available for the asking from God, who is gracious partner in human life, *"who gives to all generously and ungrudgingly."* But the one who prays for the gift of wisdom must *"ask in faith, never doubting"* – with unwavering confidence in God's generosity and love and with certainty that God will answer one's prayer.

Excursus 3: Divine Generosity

The adverb *"ἁπλῶς"* (Jas. 1:5) appears only here in the New Testament, although its cognates *"ἁπλοῦς"* and *"ἁπλότης"* appear in the Synoptics (Matt. 6:22; Luke 11:34) and Pauline epistles (Rom. 12:8; 2 Cor. 1:12; 8:2; 9:11; 11:3; Eph. 6:5; Col. 3:22) respectively. Its precise sense is debatable and James may have chosen it because of its *"multi-valence."* The immediate context favors the meaning singly in the sense of *"without reservation"* or *"without division of will,"* in contrast to the "double-minded" people who is unable to commit. A later passage on God's giving (Jas. 1:17) lends weight to the second possible meaning, *"generously,"* with liberality or *"more expansively out of pure generosity unmingled with any selfish interest."* This meaning also fits well with James' dual concerns that God's people model God's active concern for those in need (1:27; 2:15-16) and that they resist selfish ambition and self-indulgent desire (3:14; 4:1-3). A third possibility, *"sincerely,"* *"openly,"* *"without hypocrisy,"* fits well with James' emphasis on God's absolute integrity (as does the first proposed meaning). Again, God's sincerity contrasts with the hypocrisies of those congregations that confess faith in Christ and in the one God and yet dishonor the poor and disregard their

---

appeals for assistance (Jas. 2).

"*Double-minded*" people who approach God with divided hearts and doubtful minds, "*must not expect to receive anything from the Lord.*" Their hesitancy in asking stands in contrast to God's complete lack of hesitancy in giving – "*gives to all generously and ungrudgingly.*" Moreover, the doubter's indecisiveness, or "*double-mindedness*," stands in contrast to the wholeness and integrity that is James' hope for Christian life.

James 1:9 ~ 11 → Poverty and Riches

NIV	TT
[9] Believers in humble circumstances ought to take pride in their high position. [10] But the rich should take pride in their humiliation— since they will pass away like a wild flower. [11] For the sun rises with scorching heat and withers the plant; its blossom falls and its beauty is destroyed. In the same way, the rich will fade away even while they go about their business.	[9] Let the believer who is lowly boast in being raised up, [10] and the rich in being brought low, because the rich will disappear like a flower in the field. [11] For the sun rises with its scorching heat and **withers**[7] the fields; its flower falls, and its beauty perishes. It is the same way with the rich; in the midst of a busy life, they will wither away.

If vv.2-8 exhorts readers to a certain perception of testing based on what they *"know"* (v.3), this text provides the content of that knowledge.

- **9 – 11** It may be no coincidence that James' fist reference to poverty and riches is juxtaposed with words about experiences of trial. Indeed, a close reading of this letter suggests that economic hardship may have been among the chief trials with which James' first readers struggled (cf. 2:1-7, 24-27; 4:13-5:6). Here, James' words aim primarily to offer encouragement to

---

[7] **Withered Flowers** → The image of quickly wilting wildflowers (Isa. 40:6-8) recurs in the Hebrew Bible as a metaphor for transitory life (cf. Jas. 4:14). For Isaiah, what remains forever is God's word, which in context is God's hope-filled message of return for the oppressed exiles.

the lowly "*believer*" in the midst of such hardship. Interestingly, *the* "*rich*" are not explicitly referred to as "*believers*"!

The main difficulty is deciding whether the rich person is a member of the community or an outsider. If the rich person is one who oppresses the community (cf. 2:6; 5:1-6), then James' tone here must be ironic. People like this boast, even though God's reversal of status will destroy them and their riches! If the rich person is also a "*brother*" in the community, the character of this person's exaltation and the point of passing away are less clear. There are two possibilities. One is to read the sentence prophetically: Rich members of the community are not truly so, for they live by the world's values. They will be humbled for giving in to the "*testing*" of wealth and placing reliance on it. This fits James' position in 5:1-6. Another possibility is that James is making a sapiential point: The rich person is humbled within a community of the poor that does not give wealth a special status, but honors the poor instead. This fits James' argument in 4:13-17.

More important is to understand that James is not here making an exhortation, but stating basic principles concerning the human condition before God. In that light, the harsher reading is more likely, for it makes the contrast clearer. This reading is strengthened further by James' allusion to Isa. 40:7 in v.11, which suggests a contrast between reliance on appearances and on "*the word of our God will stand forever*" (Isa. 40:8). Humans live before God who exalts those who are lowly and resists those who are proud. This theme will recur in 4:6.

James 1:12~18 → God's Role in Trials and Temptations

NIV	TT
[12] Blessed is the one who perseveres under trial because, having stood the test, that person will receive the crown of life that the Lord has promised to those who love him. [13] When tempted, no one should say, "God is tempting me." For God cannot be tempted by evil, nor does he tempt anyone; [14] but each person is tempted when they are dragged away by their own evil desire and enticed. [15] Then, after desire has conceived, it gives birth to sin; and sin, when it is full-grown, gives birth to death. [16] Don't be deceived, my	[12] Blessed anyone who endures **test**[8]. Such a one has stood the test and will receive the **crown**[9] of life that the Lord has promised to those who love him. [13] No one, when **tempted**[10], should say, "I am being tempted by God"; for God cannot be tempted by evil and He Himself tempts no one. [14] But one is tempted by one's own **desire**[11], being lured and enticed by it; [15] then, when that desire has conceived, it gives birth to sin, and that sin, when it is fully grown, gives birth to death. [16] Do not be deceived, my beloved. [17] Every generous act of giving, with every perfect

---

[8] πειρασμός → The term means *"trial,"* *"temptation,"* *"test,"* *"enticement to sin,"* and *"way of tempting."*

[9] στέφανος → It means *"crown,"* *"wreath,"* *"pride,"* *"prize,"* and *"reward."* (See Excursus 4: Crown)

[10] πειράζω → The word means *"try,"* *"tempt,"* and *"entice to sin."*

[11] ἐπιθυμία → It means *"desire,"* *"longing,"* *"craving,"* and *"defiling passion."*

dear brothers and sisters. [17] Every good and perfect gift is from above, coming down from the Father of the heavenly lights, who does not change like shifting shadows. [18] He chose to give us birth through the word of truth, that we might be a kind of firstfruits of all he created.	gift, is from above, coming down from the Father of lights, with whom there is no variation or shadow due to change. [18] In fulfillment of his own purpose he gave us birth by the word of truth, so that we would become a kind of **firstfruits**[12] of his creatures.

James' discussion on trials continues, but another element is introduced. While joyful consequences of trials accrue to believers in the present (1:2-4), James now adds to this the prospect of future reward. Those who endure trials may also rejoice that they will share in the life of the age to come.

- **12 – 16** A further dimension of trial is developed in the verses that follow. The author uses the same Greek "πειρασμός," which can be rendered as "*trial*" or "*temptation.*" James now turns from the external pressures that we endure ("*trials*") to the internal impulses to sin ("*temptations*"). And what is it that draws us to sin? Make no mistake about it: Temptation is not to be blamed on God! There is nobody to blame but ourselves. We are tempted, lured, and enticed to sin not by God but by our own desire. James describes the dreadful consequences of desire: "*When that desire has conceived, it gives birth to sin, and that sin, when it is*

---

[12] ἀπαρχή → It means "*firstfruits,*" "*the first of any crop or offspring of livestock,*" and "*foretaste.*" (See Excursus 5: Firstfruits)

fully grown, gives birth to death." The source is in human desire. The word "*desire*" may carry sexual overtones but not necessarily; it can also be translated "*covet*" or "*desire to posses.*" The writer, however, does find sexual desire an appropriate image to characterize the downward slide of the one who does not endure.

Excursus 4: Crown

The term, "*στέφανος*" (crown) appears 18 times in the New Testament. There are three related ideas communicated with the word. It can refer to a physical crown or wreath worn by someone of high status. In the Greco-Roman world, a crown (often a woven wreath) was given as a sign of honor to people of high status. One such group of admired people was the victors of athletic games. Paul picks up on this usage to contrast perishable athletic crowns with the imperishable reward of obedience to Christ (1 Cor. 9:25; 2 Tim. 2:5; 4:8). Besides athletes, notable public servants and high-ranking officials were also given crowns as a sign of honor – a usage reflected in Rev. 4:4, 10; 6:2; 12:1; 14:14. This same sense is used in a mocking way by the soldiers who make a "*στέφανος*" of thorns (along with a purple robe) for Jesus (Matt. 27:29; Mark 15:17; John 19:2, 5). For the NT writers, there is a great irony here, for Jesus is in fact the true King of kings.

The other two ideas communicated by "*στέφανος*" are metaphorical. It can refer to an adornment or source of pride. In Phil. 4:1 and 1 Thess. 2:19, it is used in the sense of "*to be proud of.*" Paul speaks of his spiritual children in Philippi and Thessalonica as his joy and crown before God (cf. the gray head as a "*crown of glory*" in Prov. 16:31).

"*στέφανος*" can also mean "*prize,*" and "*reward.*" In

James 1:12 the *"crown of life"* (i.e., eternal life) is given to the one who perseveres under trial, and in 1 Pet. 5:4, faithful shepherd-elders are promised an unfading *"crown of glory"* (i.e., eternal honor). Similarly, in Rev. 2:10 the *"crown of life"* is promised to those who overcome tribulation. In each instance the emphasis is on *"of life"* and *"of glory."* The crown or reward is in fact the life or the glory promised. The use of *"στέφανος"* in such phrases heightens the drama and paints a wonderful word picture of the beauty of one who has faithfully and painfully endured and now stands on the victor's platform with joy.

- **17 – 18** Far from leading us into sin and death, God wishes to lead us into life. James underlines this fact by drawing attention to the good gifts that come from God and to the constancy of God's goodness and love: *"Every generous act of giving, with every perfect gift, is from above, coming down from the Father of lights, with whom there is no variation or shadow due to change."* Thus, God gives *"wisdom"* (v.5), *"the crown of life"* (v.12) and the writer now speaks of God as the source of all gifts. To think of life and its resources as gifts of God is important for both rich and poor.

  James draws on a creation metaphor (that is, figurative expression) in referring to God as the *"Father of lights"* – the Creator of the stars. 1st century people observed with keen interest the movements of the heavenly bodies and their waxing and waning. James affirms that their Creator and governor is exalted above any such change. Unlike the created heavenly bodies that shift in position and are darkened by the shadows of eclipse, God neither changes nor is changed by anything outside God's own self. As a familiar hymn, *"Great is Thy Faithfulness,"* puts it, *"there is no shadow of turning with thee."* For this reason, it cannot be said that God, the giver of good gifts, could also inflict evils upon us (such as *"temptation"*). Such change would be contrary to the nature of God, whose constancy is one of goodness and love.

James rests this case by providing a premier example of God's goodness: *"In fulfillment of [God's] own purpose [God] gave us birth by the word of truth, so that we would become a kind of first fruits of [God's] creatures."* James refers to the rebirth, or conversion, of Christians, who have been *"given birth"* by the *"word of truth"* (*"the gospel"* in Col 1:5) and who are *"a kind of first fruits,"* or foretaste, of the redemption of the whole created order that is to come. The life that God benevolently *"brings forth"* for us stands in marked contrast to the destruction *"brought forth"* by our own desire and sin. James states unambiguously that God's constant, unchanging will for us is not trial or temptation, but life – a life of steadfast faith and wholeness, and in the end, life eternal – a life of constancy and integrity, which is modeled on the very constancy and integrity of God.

Excursus 5: Firstfruits

The Hebrew word, "רֵאשִׁית" appears 51 times in the Old Testament. It indicates the *"beginning"* of something. But another common use of this noun is for *"the firstfruits."*

The term "*ἀπαρχή*" (firstfruits) appears 9 times in the New Testament. Since the time of the OT the Israelites were to bring the first part of a harvest as a gift to the Lord (Exod. 23:19; Neh. 10:35). By doing so they acknowledged that the harvest was provided by God and that their act of bring the firstfruits expressed faith that the rest of the harvest would follow.

"*ἀπαρχή*" is used figuratively by NT writers. Israel was and continues to be part of God's salvation history; they were his original people. "*If the dough offered as firstfruits is holy, so is the whole lump, and if the root is holy, so are the branches*" (Rom. 11:16). The first converts of a particular regin are called "firstfruits" (1 Cor. 16:15; 1 Thess. 2:3). In a more general sense, Christians are the "*firstfruits*," who are important in God's new created order. Speaking of God, James 1:18 says, "*In fulfillment of his own purpose he gave us birth by the word of truth, so that we would become a kind of firstfruits of his creatures*" (cf. Rev. 14:4).

In Rom. 8:23, Paul reverses the OT use of "*ἀπαρχή*" by describing Christians (and not God) as the ones who receive the "firstfruits" of the Spirit. The Spirit is the first installment of God's assured final redemption of the body. In a similar end-time context, Paul speaks of Christ's resurrection as the "*firstfruits*" of the final resurrection of the dead (1 Cor. 15:20, 23). Thus, the hope of the believer's resurrection from the dead is as assured as Christ's own resurrection, since Christ's resurrection is the "*ἀπαρχή*" of the resurrection to be realized at the consummation of the ages.

James 1:19~21 → Receiving the Word

NIV	TT
[19] My dear brothers and sisters, take note of this: Everyone should be quick to listen, slow to speak and slow to become angry, [20] because human anger does not produce the righteousness that God desires. [21] Therefore, get rid of all moral filth and the evil that is so prevalent and humbly accept the word planted in you, which can save you.	[19] You must **understand**[13] this, my beloved: let everyone be quick to listen, slow to speak, slow to anger; [20] for your anger does not produce God's righteousness. [21] Therefore rid yourselves of all sordidness and rank growth of wickedness, and welcome with meekness the implanted word that has the power to save your souls.

In this text, James describes the first state of response to the call implied by God's gift. The *"implanted word"* can only save them if it is truly received.

- **19 – 21** This section of James opens with a threefold appeal: *"Let everyone be quick to listen, slow to speak, slow to anger."* James values listening, temperate speech, and humility in all areas of life. In particular, however, we are urged to *"be quick to listen, slow to speak, slow to anger"* as we come before the *"word of truth"* (v.18) – *"the implanted word"* that has the power to save our lives (v.21). That word is none other than the word of the gospel, that is, God's word to us or

---

[13] Ἴστε → It means *"know," "understand," "come to know," "recognize,"* and *"remember."* It is an imperative form.

mercy, power, and renewal in Jesus Christ. One of our primary and ongoing tasks as Christians is to attend to that word as it comes to us in preaching and the sacraments, in teaching, in tradition, and in careful study of the scriptures. It is an urgent task ("*be quick to listen*"), and where Christians are thus engaged they will be "*slow to speak.*" They must listen carefully and patiently to God before they presume to speak and act in God's name.

Moreover, James urges Christians to "*rid themselves*" of anything that hinders reception of God's word. James refers to the gospel as an "*implanted word,*" for just as the sower in Jesus' parable faithfully sows the word (Mark 4), so has the word, through the preaching and teaching of many faithful witnesses, been implanted in our lives. It is James' hope that we will come to the word with openness and, through careful attention to it, nurture its growth in our lives.

James 1:22~25 → Doing the Word

NIV	TT
[22] Do not merely listen to the word, and so deceive yourselves. Do what it says. [23] Anyone who listens to the word but does not do what it says is like someone who looks at his face in a mirror [24] and, after looking at himself, goes away and immediately forgets what he looks like. [25] But whoever looks intently into the perfect law that gives freedom, and continues in it—not forgetting what they have heard, but doing it— they will be blessed in what they do.	[22] But be doers of the word, and not merely hearers who deceive themselves. [23] For it any are hearers of the word and not doers, they are like those who look at themselves in a mirror; [24] for they look at themselves and, on going away, immediately forget what they were like. [25] But those who look into the perfect law, the law of liberty, and persevere, being not hearers who forget but doers who act – they will be blessed in their doing.

The basic point is one that has been implicit from James' statement that faith can produce a perfect effect (v.4): For faith to be real, it must be translated into deeds. It is not enough to be a "*hearer of the word*" one must become a "*doer of the word*" as well. The joining of hearing and doing echoes teaching of Jesus (Matt. 7:24-27; Luke 11:28).

- **22 – 25** In James' view, the faithful hearing of the word leads to the doing of it, for receptive hearing involves commitment and obedience to what has been heard. It is important to note that James does not contrast hearers and doers, but rather compares two kinds of hearers:

those who act upon what they have heard and those who do not. *"Hearers"* always precedes *"doing"* and is the foundation for it. *"Hearers"* directs and empowers our response to God's word. Nevertheless, once we have received the implanted word and have been renewed, directed, and empowered by it, we are expected to bloom.

To make this point, James draws on a striking, though puzzling, illustration. Those who are hearers of the word, but not doers, are compared to *"those who look at themselves in a mirror"* then immediately forget their image once they have stepped away. (See Excursus 6: Ancient Mirrors) Perhaps James' point is that they look into the mirror and see that changes in their appearance are called for, but they fail to make the necessary alterations – they step away with hair still unkempt and clothes askew. Or perhaps James thinks that they look into the mirror and see grace and forgiveness reflected there, but the impression is only fleeting, and they step away from the newness of life that has been wrought by the word. Whichever the case, hearing that does not lead to doing is worthless. Those who come before God's word in this manner are deceiving themselves if they think that they have really heard (v.22).

Excursus 6: Ancient Mirrors

In the New Testament world mirrors were a luxury item. Highly polished bronze mirrors were labor intensive products; *"high end"* end mirrors were fashioned from silver and often featured elaborate

---

gilded decoration. James' appeal to the image of the mirror may be a subtle jab at those rich enjoying consumptive lifestyles. They (or their servants) adjust their hair based on what they see in the mirror but they do not see themselves in the scripture's call to adjust their lives to sow active concern for those in need.

These *"hearers who forget"* are contrasted with those who hear the word, attend to it, persevere in it, and act upon it – those who translate the implications of the gospel into their lives. The word is referred to as *"law"* (v.25), because once received, it implies commitment and obedience. Moreover, the *"law"* to which James refers is none other than the will of God for our lives as revealed in the Old Testament and in the life and teaching of Jesus Christ. That will, or *"law,"* is *"perfect"* because it is complete, lacking in nothing (compare 1:4), and because it leads therefore to the *"perfection"* or *"maturity"* or *"wholeness"* that is James' hope for Christian life. It is also referred to as a "law of liberty," because it liberates us from false slaveries and desires (1:14-15) and has the power to save our souls (v.21).

Cosmetics magnate Estee Lauder insists that *"a good mirror is the most important accessory in a woman's life."* Since I am not a female, I may be able to agree with her fully. However, all of us – men and women – need a good mirror that will help us see ourselves as we really are. James reminds us that there is only one mirror that shows forth our true reflection: the gospel of Jesus Christ. In that mirror, which James holds before us, we see who we are in the light of God's love and what we are meant to be.

James 1:26~27 → Genuine Religion

NIV	TT
[26] Those who consider themselves religious and yet do not keep a tight rein on their tongues deceive themselves, and their religion is worthless. [27] Religion that God our Father accepts as pure and faultless is this: to look after orphans and widows in their distress and to keep oneself from being polluted by the world.	[26] If any think they are religious, and do not bridle their tongues but deceive their hearts, their **religion**[14] is worthless. [27] Religion that is pure and undefiled before God, the Father, is this: to care for orphans and widows in their distress, and to keep oneself unstained by the world.

As the popular novelist and theologian Frederick Buechner observes, many people think of religion as "*a good think, like social security and regular exercise,*" but not "*something to go overboard about.*" But to James' way of thinking, religion is not a casual matter. It calls for serious commitment, both in terms of careful "*hearing*" and faithful "*doing.*"

- **26 – 27** In James' view, genuinely religious people are "*doers of the word, and not hearers only.*" But of what does authentic religious activity consist? James makes three concrete suggestions. First, right hearing of

---

[14] θρησκεία → It means "*religion,*" and "*worship.*" It is a rare word in the New Testament. It appears in Acts 26:5 and Col. 2:18.Religion that is meaningful rather than empty must have the integrity of word and work.

God's word is never without effect on our speaking –
on what we say and how we speak to one another.
Indeed, James suggests that *"if any think they are*
religious, and do not bridle their tongues but deceive
their hearts, their religion is worthless." Right hearing
of the word empowers us for self-control and, in James'
view, nowhere is self-control more urgently needed
than in our speaking (cf. James 3).

Second, genuine religion consists of caring *"for*
orphans and widows in their distress." In so advising,
James stands squarely in the tradition of the Hebrew
scriptures, in which widows and orphans are frequently
lifted up as representative of the oppressed and as a
special focus of God's concern (cf. Isa. 1:16-17). For
James, too, they are representative of all who find
themselves defenseless and suffering poverty, distress,
and oppression. Genuine religion is marked by care
and concern for people in need.

Finally, genuine religion consists of keeping oneself
"unstained by the world." In so advising, James by no
means suggests that Christians are to refrain from
involvement in the world. Has it not just commended
attention to those in need? Rather, the author
encourages Christians to take full part in the affairs of
the world but not to embrace the world's standards.
James uses the term *"world"* to refer to ways of
thinking and systems of values that do not take God's
existence and God's claims into account. Christians are
to be engaged in the world, but they are to hold a
different understanding of reality and a different set of

values, informed by their experience of the grace of God in Jesus Christ.

The same viewpoint is reflected in the words of Jesus in the Gospel of John, where it speaks of Christians as being "*in the world*" but "*not of the world*" (John 17:14-18). Similarly, the apostle Paul urges us Christians not to be "*conformed to this world*" but to be "*transformed*" by the renewing of our minds, that we may "*discern what is the will of God – what is good and acceptable and perfect*" (Rom. 12:2).

Religion, then, is a great deal more than doctrine or rituals, although it includes these. In the final analysis – for James at least – the test of genuine religion is not orthodoxy ("*right belief*") but orthopraxy ("*right practice*").

James 2:1~4 → Warning Against Discrimination

NIV	TT
2 ¹ My brothers and sisters, believers in our glorious Lord Jesus Christ must not show favoritism. ² Suppose a man comes into your meeting wearing a gold ring and fine clothes, and a poor man in filthy old clothes also comes in. ³ If you show special attention to the man wearing fine clothes and say, "Here's a good seat for you," but say to the poor man, "You stand there" or "Sit on the floor by my feet," ⁴ have you not discriminated among	2 ¹ My brothers and sisters, do you with your acts of favoritism[15] really **faith in our glorious Lord Jesus Christ**?[16] ² For if a person with gold rings and in fine clothes comes into your **synagogue,**[17] and a poor person in dirty clothes also comes in, ³ and if you take notice of the one wearing the fine clothes and say, "Have a seat here, please," while to the one who is poor you say, "Stand there," or, "Sit at my feet," ⁴ have you not made distinctions among

[15] προσωπολημψία → It means *"partiality," "respect of people,"* and *"personal favoritism."* This word have so far been found only in Christian writers.

[16] ἢν πίστιν τοῦ κυρίου ἡμῶν Ἰησοῦ Χριστοῦ τῆς δόξης → The phrase can be translated as a subjective genitive, *"The faith of our glorious Lord Jesus Christ"* (the faith that Jesus displayed) or as an objective genitive *"The faith in our glorious Lord Jesus Christ."*

[17] συναγωγὴν → Many translate this term as *"assembly," "meeting," "congregation,"* and *"gathering."* However, literally it is *"synagogue."* James is the most Jewish of all the New Testament writings. James here uses the word *"synagogue"* for the Jewish-Christian assembly or its meeting house (2:2); later James uses the term *"church,"* or *"ecclesia"* for the local congregation (5:14). James' mixed usage may suggest communities that are comfortable with their Jewish roots and identity.

yourselves and become judges with evil thoughts?	yourselves, and become judges with evil thoughts?

The first part of chapter 2 isolates an incident of favoritism or discrimination against a poor person. Such judgments of the poor are condemned in the Old Testament (Lev. 19:15; Psalms 82:2), and James is likewise concerned with people making distinctions among themselves.

- **1 – 4** James maintains that faith in Jesus Christ bears directly upon our treatment of people. Thus signs of snobbery and partiality in the Christian community prompt an incredulous question: *"My brothers and sisters, do you with your acts of favoritism really believe in our glorious Lord Jesus Christ?"*

  The fact that James refers to *"acts of favoritism"* in the plural form suggests that discrimination can manifest itself in the Christian community in a variety of ways. But by using a flagrant example, the author leaves no doubt as to the kind of attitude and behavior deemed incompatible with Christian faith. Two visitors are depicted as entering the faith community: one bejeweled and one bedraggled; one from the lap of luxury and the other, perhaps, from the streets. The extreme contrast in their appearance is highlighted: the bejeweled visitor is dressed in *"fine clothes"* and the poor visitor in *"dirty clothes."*

  These sharply contrasted people are given correspondingly contrasting receptions. The bejeweled visitor is treated with extreme courtesy (*"Have a seat here, please"*), while the bedraggled guest is brusquely shuffled aside (*"Stand there"* or *"Sit at my feet"*).

When Christians *"make distinctions"* among themselves in any such manner, haven't they *"become judges with evil thoughts"*? (Lev. 19:15) Are they not manifesting that internal dividedness that belies integrity of faith? By kowtowing to the counterfeit glory of the splendidly attired, have they not betrayed the truly glorious one who alone is to be exalted in the Christian community and before whom all are equal: *"our glorious Lord Jesus Christ"* (2:1)?

James 2:5~13 → Why Discrimination is Inconsistent with Christian Faith

NIV	TT
[5] Listen, my dear brothers and sisters: Has not God chosen those who are poor in the eyes of the world to be rich in faith and to inherit the kingdom he promised those who love him? [6] But you have dishonored the poor. Is it not the rich who are exploiting you? Are they not the ones who are dragging you into court? [7] Are they not the ones who are blaspheming the noble name of him to whom you belong? [8] If you really keep the royal law found in Scripture, "Love your neighbor as yourself," you are doing right. [9] But if you show favoritism, you sin and are convicted by the law as lawbreakers. [10] For whoever keeps the whole law and yet stumbles at just one point is guilty of breaking all of it. [11] For he who said, "You shall not commit adultery,"	[5] Listen, my beloved brothers and sisters. Has not God chosen the poor in the world to be rich in faith and to be heirs of the kingdom that He has promised to those who love him? [6] But you have dishonored the poor. Is it not the rich who oppress you? Is it not they who drag you into court? [7] Is it not they who blaspheme the excellent name that was invoked over you? [8] You do well if you really fulfill the royal law according to the scripture, "you shall love your neighbor as yourself." [9] But if you show favoritism, you commit sin and are convicted by the law as transgressors. [10] For whoever keeps the whole law but fails in one point has become accountable for all of it. [11] For the one who said, "You shall not commit adultery," also said, "You

also said, "You shall not murder." If you do not commit adultery but do commit murder, you have become a lawbreaker.	shall not murder." Now if you do not commit adultery but if you murder, you have become a transgressor of the law.
[12] Speak and act as those who are going to be judged by the law that gives freedom, [13] because judgment without mercy will be shown to anyone who has not been merciful. Mercy triumphs over judgment.	[12] So speak and so act as those who are to be judged by the law of liberty. [13] For judgment will be without mercy to anyone who has shown no mercy; mercy triumphs over judgment.

Though Christians have experienced oppression by the rich, they have learned from their oppressors, not from God! The tendency of the oppressed to adopt the behavior of their oppressors frequently emerges in revolutionary movements. The lowly may prefer the limited power they can exercise against others to the exaltation that comes from God. Religious leadership must insist on the equality of all people as children of God.

- **5 – 7** To James' way of thinking, the kind of snobbery depicted in verses 2-4 is far from a trivial matter. In fact, the author proceeds to establish three grounds on which "*acts of favoritisms*" constitute a serious denial of faith.

    First, he reminds his readers of God's special care and concern for the poor (v.5) – a concern that is stressed throughout the scriptures (cf. Luke 6:20). It should be clear, then, that when members of the

Christian community ignore the poor, they are not reflecting God's compassion. When they slight the poor, they dishonor those whom God has honored, whom God has "*chosen*" to be "*rich in faith*" and "*heirs of the kingdom*." How is it that the prejudices of the world rather than the preferences of God come to be manifested in a community of God's people?

Second, the author appeals to his readers' own experiences. He suggests that "*acts of favoritism*" make little sense in light of the way they themselves are treated at the hands of the rich: "*Is it not the rich who oppress you? Is it not they who drag you into court? Is it not they who blaspheme the excellent name that was invoked over you?*"

James' letter reflects a time when people of wealth were not yet often found in the Christian community – at least not in the communities with which the author was most closely associated. Members of the Christian community may very well have been taken to court by the rich over such issues as debts, rents, and wages (see 5:4-6). As a result, they may also have found themselves the objects of slander and popular gossip on the part of the rich – disparaged as bad citizens or unreliable debtors. James regards any such treatments as blasphemy, for Christians bear the name of Jesus from the moment they are baptized in the name of Christ (cf. Acts 2:38). In James' view, abuse of those who bear the name of Christ is abuse of Christ himself. Thus it is bewildering that members of the Christian community should grovel before those who exploit the poor, harass Christians, and dishonor Christ.

- **8 – 11** Third, the author insists that favoritism toward the rich is also a transgression of the biblical principle of love. Readers are reminded of the familiar commandment to *"love your neighbor as yourself"* (Lev. 19:18). This commandment, in fact, is referred to as the *"royal law,"* because it is the law of the kingdom into which God has called them (cf. Mark 12:29-31).

    Those whom James addresses may very well have argued, as do we, that in attending to the rich they are showing love to their neighbors. And if this is really the case, then they *"do well."* But this is no excuse for favoritism. If in attending to the rich, readers discriminate against the poor, then they *"commit sin and are convicted by the law as transgressors"* (v.9). They have not understood that the poor person whom they dishonor is also a neighbor and that *"acts of favoritism"* place them in violation of the biblical commandment to love.

    Moreover, *"acts of favoritism"* are not to be dismissed as minor infractions of God's command – as misdemeanors rather than felonies. In order to underline the seriousness of the crime of partiality, James draws on the ancient Jewish doctrine of the complete unity of the law and contends that to violate the law at this one point is to break the law as a whole (v.10; cf. Gal. 5:3). To illustrate this point, James links partiality with the heinous sins of adultery and murder – sins readers would not fail to consider serious. Adulterers will not suppose that they should be excused of adultery because they have not committed murder (v.11). James' point is that the adulterer stands guilty before the law, as does the murderer – and as does the one who discriminates. God, who forbids adultery and murder, also forbids discrimination. God stands behind every commandment. Thus, all three – the adulterer, the murderer, and the one who commits *"acts of favoritism"* – are transgressors of the law and are subject to God's judgment.

- **12 – 13** In closing, James remind us all that we are accountable to God for our words and deeds (v.12). At the lad day, every individual will stand before the judgment seat of God. What will be determined at that point is not whether we are to be *"saved"*; we have already been saved by the grace of God through faith in Jesus Christ. What the judgment will reveal is whether or not we have misused the grace that is ours – whether or not we have embodied in our lives the possibilities the gospel offers. Our practice of indiscriminate love toward all people will reveal whether we have allowed the grace and power of God to produce a transformation in our lives. Impartiality in all our doings is, in no small part, a sign of the integrity of faith.

Excursus 7: Law of Liberty

Several distinct streams of early Christian tradition viewed Christ as one bringing freedom, often time through his distinctive teaching. In Matthew 11:29-30, Jesus' reinterpretation of the Torah is an easy yoke and a light burden, in contrast to the Pharisees' oral tradition that weighed heavily on the *"people of the land."* Within the Johannine tradition, Jesus' *"commandments are not burdensome"* (1 John 5:3). Chief among these commandments is that of love for

---

> community members (1 John 4:21). Within the Pauline corpus, Christian freedom is an opportunity to *"through love become slaves to one another"* (Gal. 5:13-14). Bearing one another's burdens fulfills *"the law of Christ"* (Gal. 6:2).

Clearly, James has much to contribute to our thinking about acts and experiences of discrimination. Indeed, Howard University scholar Cain Hope Felder observes that James 2:1-13 provides what is perhaps the strongest castigation of class discrimination in the New Testament – or for that matter, any discrimination based on outward appearance – and that these words have particular pertinence for African Americans who still experience such discrimination daily.

The fact that James speaks of *"acts of favoritism"* (plural!) should prompt us to ponder all those experiences in which we have made snap judgments about others on the basis of outward appearance – perhaps on the basis of disability, dress, race, class, gender, or age. From James' perspective, discrimination of any kind is simply inconsistent with Christian faith.

James 2:14~26 → Faith and Works

NIV	TT
[14] What good is it, my brothers and sisters, if someone claims to have faith but has no deeds? Can such faith save them? [15] Suppose a brother or a sister is without clothes and daily food. [16] If one of you says to them, "Go in peace; keep warm and well fed," but does nothing about their physical needs, what good is it? [17] In the same way, faith by itself, if it is not accompanied by action, is dead. [18] But someone will say, "You have faith; I have deeds." Show me your faith without deeds, and I will show you my faith by my deeds. [19] You believe that there is one God. Good! Even the	[14] What good is it, my brothers and sisters, if someone claims to have faith but has no deeds? Can such faith **save**[18] them? [15] Suppose a brother or a sister is without clothes and daily food. [16] If one of you says to them, "Go in peace; keep warm and well fed," but does nothing about their physical needs, what good is it? [17] So faith by itself, if it has no works, is dead. [18] But someone will say, "You have faith; I have deeds." Show me your faith without deeds, and I will show you my faith by my deeds. [19] You believe that there is one God. Good! Even the **demons**[19] believe that—and shudder. [20] You **empty fellow**[20], do you want evidence that faith

---

[18] σῴζω → It means "*rescue*," "*liberate*," "*heal*," "*preserve*," "*attain salvation*," and "*make whole*."

[19] δαιμόνιον → It means "*deity*," "*divinity*," "*demon*," and "*evil spirit*."

[20] ὦ ἄνθρωπε κενε → This means "*empty man*," "*foolish person*," "*senseless fellow*" or "*hallow man*."

demons believe that—and shudder.

20 You foolish person, do you want evidence that faith without deeds is useless? 21 Was not our father Abraham considered righteous for what he did when he offered his son Isaac on the altar? 22 You see that his faith and his actions were working together, and his faith was made complete by what he did. 23 And the scripture was fulfilled that says, "Abraham believed God, and it was credited to him as righteousness," and he was called God's friend. 24 You see that a person is considered righteous by what they do and not by faith alone.

25 In the same way, was not even Rahab the prostitute considered righteous for what she did when she gave lodging to the spies and sent apart from works is empty? 21 Was not our father Abraham shown to be righteous for what he did when he offered his son Isaac on the altar? 22 You see that his faith co-worked the work, and his faith was brought to fulfillment by the deed. 23 And the scripture was fulfilled that says, "Abraham believed God, and it was credited to him as righteousness," and he was called the **Friend of God**[21]. 24 You see that a person is **justified**[22] by works and not by faith alone. 25 In the same way, was not even Rahab the prostitute considered righteous for what she did when she gave lodging to the spies and sent them off in a different direction? 26 As the body without the spirit is dead, so faith without deeds is dead.

---

[21] φίλος θεοῦ → The phrase means *"associate of God," "companion of God,"* and *"friend of God."*
[22] δικαιόω → It means *"justify," "vindicate,"* and *"treat as just."*

them off in a different direction? [26] As the body without the spirit is dead, so faith without deeds is dead.	

This unit falls naturally into two parts: the first (vv.14-17) consists of a series of questions and a concluding piece of proverbial wisdom; the second (vv.18-26) consists of a series of arguments concluding with a repetition of the proverb in verse 17.

- **14 – 17** James starts with the question of usefulness (2:14). How can faith that is professed but is not manifested in deeds ("*works*") be authentic? Even though he uses the term "*save*" in the question, "*Can faith save you?*" (2:14), James' topic is not really soteriology; he has already declared that it is the "*implanted word*" from God that "*is able to save your souls*" (1:21). The issue is, rather, how to be a "*doer*" of that word. Notice furthermore that James does not talk here about the "*works of the law*" but specifically about the "*works of faith*." His topic is the necessary unity between attitude and action that preoccupies the moralists of his and virtually every age. The point is certainly not that the actions substitute for the attitude! It is, rather, that the actions reveal the attitude and make it "*alive*." As interpreters from Origen to Calvin recognized, James' position is precisely that expressed by Paul in Gal. 5:6, "*neither circumcision nor uncircumcision counts for anything; the only thing that counts is faith working through love.*"

It is within such a moral framework that this section of James should be understood. His opening illustration provides the negative example and bears strong resemblance to the admonition in 1 John 3:17-18. The "*brothers and sisters*" are obviously among the poorest of the poor, lacking both clothes and daily food. Furthermore, their condition cannot be missed; the believer sees them and speaks to them. But they are dismissed with kind wishes and religious jargon (2:15-16). This is the perfect illustration of the "*empty religion*" that James rejects, combining self-indulgence, failure to control the tongue, and a refusal to care for orphans and widows (1:27). It is, therefore, not "*unstained by the world*" or "*pure and undefiled before God.*" James declares such purported faith to be, simply, "*dead*" (2:17).

- **18 – 26** James' response is an insistence on the indivisibility of the two: One can "*show*" faith by pointing to the deeds of faith. But what would faith look like without any deeds? James suggests that it would be simply "*belief*," as an intellectual assent: There is one God. His response is ironic: God for you! But the inadequacy of such "*faith*" is obvious when one considers that even those forces that oppose God have that level of belief, without responding to God positively at all (2:19). This is a parody of faith rather than the response of those who love God (1:12; 2:5).

In 2:20 James uses apostrophe and a rhetorical question with a fine sense of irony. His interlocutor is an "*empty fellow*," who will be shown how faith "*apart from works is empty.*" His own understanding of genuine faith is found in the examples he cites from Torah (2:20-25). Both Abraham and Rahab had faith that was demonstrated by their actions. James' choice of the testing of Abraham (Gen. 22:1-18) is particularly appropriate, for Abraham's obedience was precisely an act of faith. In a sentence whose Greek is much clearer than either the NIV or the NRSV translation, James insists that the faith *"co-worked the work"* and that faith was *"brought to perfection/fulfillment"* by the deed (2:22). In other words, faith is the subject from the beginning to end. Deeds do not replace faith; they complete it.

Like Paul, James cites Gen. 15:6, which declares Abraham righteous because of his faith. But James' way of understanding that verse is a bit different; for James, Abraham's willingness to sacrifice his son in obedience to God was itself the *"fulfillment"* of the text in Gen. 15:6. Thus the translation of 2:21 might better be that Abraham was *"shown to be righteous,"* since the entire line of argumentation has involved demonstration. And it is in the light of James' own demonstration – rather than as a response to Paul on a completely different controversy – that his declaration in v.24 should be understood. If *"works"* are understood as the *"works/deeds"* of faith itself – that is, as the expression of faith itself in acts of obedience – then it seems plainly the case that, as he says, a person is declared righteous on the basis of deeds and not only on faith. Distinctive to James' treatment of Abraham is his designation of him as *"friend of God."* This is not part of the Genesis citation, but seems to derive from a merging of the statements in 2 Chr. 20:7 and Isa. 41:8 that God "*loved*" Abraham and the Hellenistic understanding of friendship as a peculiarly close sharing of all material and spiritual things. "*Friends,*" said the Greeks, "*are of one mind.*"[23] For James to call Abraham "*friend of God*" because of his offering of Isaac fits within the dualistic framework of his composition. We have seen him opposing the measure/wisdom of the world with that from God (cf. 2:5). This opposition reaches its most explicit form in 4:4, where James will contrast "*friendship with the world*" and "*friendship with God*" as antithetical options.

Abraham represents the person who is not double-minded and truly "*wills one things.*" He thinks and acts according to the measure of God. If Abraham had been a "*friend of the world,*" then he would not have been willing to sacrifice his son. He would have viewed reality as a closed system in which his future was determined by what he could possess and control. Even though Isaac was a gift from God, he was not "*Abraham's*" and his way of securing the promise. Thinking in worldly terms, Abraham's killing his son when he had no human hope for another would be folly. But Abraham showed he was a friend of God, because he considered God to be One who gives to all generously and without grudging (1:5), the giver of every good and perfect gift (1:7), who gives to the humble a greater gift (4:6). Abraham saw things God's

---

[23] See, Euripides *Orestes* 1046; Aristotle *Nicomanchean Ethics* 1168b.

way: If God could give Isaac as a gift, then God could give another gift also. Abraham's willingness to give back to God what God had gifted him with demonstrates and perfects his faith and shows what "*friendship with God*" means.

The example of Rahab takes only one verse (2:25), but is noteworthy first of all because it provides a straightforward female exemplar from Torah – a woman who is to be imitated for her own behavior and not because of her relationship to a patriarch. Rahab's story is recounted in Josh. 2:2-21, and in Jewish lore shoe was celebrated above all as a proselyte and as an example of hospitality. The combination of faith and hospitality is picked up by James. In contrast to Heb. 11:31, James does not mention her faith explicitly, but readers would remember that Rahab made a confession of the Lord as the one God in Josh. 2:16. James focuses on her reception of the Israelite scouts as an expression of that faith.

The question arises as to why Rahab is included at all, if her example is so unelaborated. This question attaches itself also to James' odd use of plural "*works*" with reference to Abraham in 2:21-22 – odd, because only one "*work*" (the binding of Isaac) is mentioned. It is possible that this plural is the clue to the subtler midrashic implications of James' inclusion of Rahab and Abraham. In the Jewish tradition, both figures were renowned above all for their hospitality. It is certainly possible that James intended the reader to catch not only that Rahab's faith was demonstrated by hospitality but that Abraham's was as well. This possibility is intriguing on two counts. First, it provides a male and a female figure to correspond to the *"brother and sister"* in dire need of hospitality (2:14-16) and who are turned away by the pious but unmerciful believer. Second, it makes the *"deeds"* of Abraham and Rahab fit the specific argument that James has been developing throughout chapter 2. The first vignette in vv.1-4 showed the poor being marginalized within the community by a lack of hospitality; the second showed the desperately needy deprived of assistance by community members. Perhaps the combined examples of Abraham and Rahab provide a response, showing how active faith demands a sharing of gifts that God has given and a providing of space to those whom God sends unexpectedly. It is significant that whereas James portrays the *"wicked judges"* (vv.2-4) as speaking, the callous believers (vv.15-16) as speaking, and the dense interlocutor (v.18) as speaking, Abraham and Rahab do not speak. Their faith is shown in action. James concludes this discussion with a final aphorism in v.26 that repeats v.17: *"Faith without deeds is dead."*

Excursus 8: Faith and Works

James is often compared to the apostle Paul, who taught that faith is based on the righteousness of God – that one is justified by faith through grace, a salvific gift from God. For Paul, works/deeds do not provide justification from God (Rom. 3:28; Gal. 2:16). But for James works/deeds are necessary, indeed foundational, for anyone claiming to have faith in God. Thus, James concludes in 2:24: *"a person is justified by works/deeds and not by faith alone."*

Both Paul and James appeal to the story of Abraham, who offered his son, Isaac, on the altar (Gen. 22:1-19), to explain their understanding of faith. Paul demonstrates the faith of Abraham from his acceptance of God's promise (Gen. 15:5-6; Rom. 4; Gal. 3:6-18); James, on the other hand, demonstrates the faith of Abraham by emphasizing the concrete action (work/deed) that was necessary in order for Abraham's faith to become complete.

For James, one can only understand the meaning of faith in the context of a community of individuals who are seeking to become mature and complete in their faith. Then I understand the examples of Abraham and Rahab as an indication that faith can be *"perfected"/"completed"* or made mature by works/deeds.

Overall, both Paul and James are needed to keep Christian faith in perspective. Paul forcefully reminds us that there is nothing we can do to *"earn"* God's grace and forgiveness. We can only accept it. This affirmation bears constant repeating, lest we fall into trap of *"works righteousness"* – of thinking that we must earn God's grace and approval with good works. James, however, forcefully reminds us that works are intrinsically related to faith and are, in fact, its proper expression. This affirmation also bears repeating, lest we proclaim *"cheap grace"* – that is, lest we forget that Christians are called to be disciples and that genuine faith finds expression in a lifestyle that is compatible with one's convictions. God's grace comes to us as mercy, and also as power for transformation of our lives!

James 3:1~5a → The Power of the Tongue

NIV	TT
3 [1] Not many of you should become teachers, my fellow believers, because you know that we who teach will be judged more strictly. [2] We all stumble in many ways. Anyone who is never at fault in what they say is perfect, able to keep their whole body in check.	3 [1] Not many of you should become teachers, my **brothers and sisters**[24], for you know that we who teach will receive the greater judgment. [2] For all of us make many mistakes. Anyone who makes no mistakes in speaking is perfect, able to keep the whole body in check with a bridle. [3] If we put bits into the mouths of horses to make them obey us, we guide their whole bodies.
[3] When we put bits into the mouths of horses to make them obey us, we can turn the whole animal. [4] Or take ships as an example. Although they are so large and are driven by strong winds, they are steered by a very small rudder wherever the pilot wants to go. [5a] Likewise, the tongue is a small part of the body, but it makes great boasts.	[4] Or look at ships: though they are so large that it takes strong winds to drive them, yet they are guided by a very small rudder wherever the will of the pilot directs. [5a] So also the tongue is a small member, yet it boasts of great exploits.

The Book of James chapter 3 consists of two interrelated periscopes, the first calling for a new perspective on the

---

[24] ἀδελφοὶ → It means "*brother,*" "*fellow countryman,*" "*neighbor,*" "*brethren,*" and "*brothers and sisters.*" (See Excursus 9: Brothers and Sisters)

tongue; the second, for a new take on wisdom. Both themes have been introduced earlier in the letter and are more fully developed in this chapter.

- **1 – 5a** The discussion of disciplined speech begins with those for whom speaking is a vocation: teachers. It is striking that for the only time in the entire Book of James, James uses the first-person plural with reference to teachers, ("*we*," v.1 – the identity of the author). *"Not many of you should become teachers, my brothers and sister, for you know that we who teach will receive the greater judgment."* The reason for this warning becomes plain as the author zeroes in on his central point of interest. While all people make mistakes, teachers are at special risk, for the tongue, the teacher's chief tool of trade, is a powerful and dangerous instrument. But all believers are implied in this dramatic portrait of the tongue.

    Of all the sins by which people stumble, those of the tongue are the most difficult to avoid. Indeed, James holds forth the ideal of the "*perfect*" person as one who makes no mistakes in what he or she says and is therefore "*able to keep the whole body in check with a bridle.*" ("*Perfection*" refers not to "*sinlessness*" but to the "*maturity*," the "*wholeness*," the "*integrity*" of Christian life; cf. 1:4). James may be suggesting that those who are able to control the tongue can certainly do that which is far easier, which is to control the body also. Or James may be suggesting that by controlling one's words, one thereby gains control of the body as a whole. Sinful deeds and impulses are often dependent upon the igniting spark of the tongue.

Whichever of these suggestions is intended, the though leads to a series of dramatic images that highlight the importance of disciplined speech. The images illustrate the astonishing potential of the tongue, which exercises a power and influence far out of proportion to its small size. Like the bit in the mouth of a horse, or like the rudder guiding a wind-tossed ship, the tongue also is small in size but great in its effect. In sum, *"the tongue is a small member, yet it boasts of great exploits."* The boast is not challenged, for James is keenly aware of the awesome power of speech.

Excursus 9: Brothers and Sisters

James, and also Paul uses this language of *"ἀδελφὸι"* – *"brothers and sisters" "brethren," "brothers"* a lot in their writings. Contemporary Christians understands this language of *"a new family"* is a Christian thing. However, Christians were heirs to the Jewish conception of the people of God as *"brothers and sisters,"* which was for Israel merely an exaggeration of natural genealogical proximity (they were, ideally at least, all actually related as descendants of Jacob). This conception of people of God as kin takes a particularly Christ-centered focus. It is now attachment to this Jesus that determines whether or not a person is in the family, rather than the person's bloodline or natural lineage. It gave the early church a sense of shared identity and bound the members together in the solidarity of the kinship bond. Also it provided them with a legitimate connection to the promises of God recounted in the Jewish Scriptures.

The critical link in the construction of this family is Jesus, who enjoys a double lineage (Rom. 1:3-4). He is a legitimate descendant of Abraham, but he is also *"the Son of God"* (Mark 1:1), and the *"heir of all things"* (Heb. 1:2) both aspects of this lineage are highly significant for the presentation of the Christian family as the true *"descendants of Abraham"* as well as *"children of God,"* the many siblings of the *"firstborn of many sisters and brothers"* (Rom. 8:29). The believers, Christians do experience their favored status as sons and daughters of God in the *"assembly,"* *"house church,"* and in their enjoyment of God's gifts.

James 3:5b~8 → The Tongue's Potential for Evil

NIV	TT
[5b] Consider what a great forest is set on fire by a small spark. [6] The tongue also is a fire, a world of evil among the parts of the body. It corrupts the whole body, sets the whole course of one's life on fire, and is itself set on fire by hell. [7] All kinds of animals, birds, reptiles and sea creatures are being tamed and have been tamed by mankind, [8] but no human being can tame the tongue. It is a restless evil, full of deadly poison.	[5b] How great a forest is set ablaze by a small fire! [6] And the tongue is a fire. The tongue is placed among our members as a world of iniquity; it stains the whole body, sets on fire the cycle of nature, and is itself set on fire by **Gehenna**[25]. [7] For every species of beast and bird, of reptile and sea creature, can be tamed and has been tamed by the human species, [8] but no one can tame the tongue – a **restless**[26] **evil**[27], full of deadly poison.

The great power of the tongue can also be used for evil purposes. This potential is clearly at the heart of James'

---

[25] γέεννα → Literally and historically, it means *"Gehenna."* *"Gehenna"* referred originally to *"the Valley of Hinnom,"* south of Jerusalem, that served as the city's garbage dump where refuse was burned. Figuratively, it became to be an image of *"a place of fire for the punishment of the wicked,"* and *"hell."* (Matt. 5:22; 18:9; Mark 9:42-48).

[26] ἀκατάσχετος → It means *"restless,"* *"unstable,"* *"uncontrollable,"* or *"inconstant."* The same term describes the *"double-minded"* person of James 1:8.

[27] κακός → It means *"bad,"* *"evil,"* *"wrong,"* and *"harmful."* (See Excursus 10: Evil)

concern, for a spiraling series of remarkable images now graphically portray the destructive effect of undisciplined speech.

- **5b – 8** The tongue is likened to a fire, which though small, is capable of wild and far-reaching devastation: *"How great a forest is set ablaze by a small fire!"* Moreover, it sets on fire the *"cycle of nature"* – a peculiar phrase with which James appears to suggest that the tongue's devastating effect is felt throughout the entire course of human life, from the cradle to the grave. And no one can tame it!

    James underscores the inability of humans to discipline their speech. Although human beings, who have been given dominion over the earth (Genesis 1), exercise mastery over the whole animal world (the four classes of animals – beast, bird, reptile, and sea creature cf. Deut. 4:17-18), they cannot master their own unruly tongues. The tongue alone is beyond control. Indeed, it is *"a restless evil, full of deadly poison,"* akin to the venomous tongue of a snake. The imagery is sever and exaggerated to be sure – the better to impress upon us the dangerous potential of uncontrolled speech.

Excursus 10: Evil

In the New Testament writings, there are various evils such as *"ἀδικία," "κακός,"* and *"πονηρόσ."* What we have in the Book of James is *"κακός."*

"κακός" appears 50 times in the New Testament, it conveys the idea of something that is *"evil," "bad," "wicked," "wrong"* – i.e., a perversion of what pertains to goodness. Generally speaking, it is a wider term.

The presence of "*κακός*" raises the question of the origin, nature, and purpose of evil in relation to God, man, and providence. In the NT good and evil are opposites, but they are not equal. Since "*God cannot be tempted by evil*" (James 1:13), the root of evil cannot lie in God. The use of "*κακός*" can be loosely divided into what is morally or ethically evil and what is destructive, damaging, or harmful.

James 3:9~12 → The Inconsistency of the Tongue

NIV	TT
[9] With the tongue we praise our Lord and Father, and with it we curse human beings, who have been made in God's likeness. [10] Out of the same mouth come praise and cursing. My brothers and sisters, this should not be. [11] Can both fresh water and salt water flow from the same spring? [12] My brothers and sisters, can a fig tree bear olives, or a grapevine bear figs? Neither can a salt spring produce fresh water.	[9] With it we **bless**[28] the Lord and Father, and with it we curse those who are made in the likeness of God. [10] From the same mouth come blessing and cursing. My brothers and sisters, this ought not to be so. [11] Does a spring pour forth from the same opening both fresh and **bitter**[29] water? [12] Can a fig tree, my brothers and sisters, yield olives, or a grapevine figs? No more can salt water yield fresh.

James motivates us to make every effort to tame the tongue. Thus it censures the inconsistency of uncontrolled speech. The tongue is fickle, and to illustrate this point James provides a specific example of inconsistent speech: *"With it we bless the Lord and Father, and with it we curse those who are made in the likeness of God. From the same mouth come blessing and cursing"* (vv. 9-10).

- **9 – 12** It is not right that the tongue be used for such incompatible activities, that it should bless God and curse human beings who have been created by God in

---

[28] εὐλογέω → It means *"speak well of," "praise," "bless," "give thanks,"* and *"request God's favor for someone."*
[29] πικρός → It means *"bitter,"* and *"harsh."*

the divine image. Such inconsistent speech is indicative of the double-mindedness condemned in 1:8 and 4:8 and is utterly inappropriate for believers.

James rests this case with an appeal to the world of nature, highlighting with a final series of images the absurdity of inconsistent speech. Such speech should be as much out of the question for the believer as it would be for a spring to yield both fresh water bitter, or for a fig tree to produce olives. Nature is not guilty of the duplicity that characterizes the human tongue. The point is inescapable: of all God's creatures, only humans violate the integrity and consistency of creation. *"This ought not to be so"* (v. 10).

These final images call us to restore integrity and discipline to Christian speech. Change is possible, in James' view, or else so much energy would not have been expended on this topic of disciplined speech. To be sure, change will not be accomplished through our own efforts alone (3:8) but in reliance upon the power of God *"who gives to all generously and ungrudgingly"* that we may be *"mature and complete"* (1:4-5).

James' reflection on the tongue may be among the most perennially relevant words in the whole letter. It bears on present-day Christian life on a variety of fronts. In recent years, for example, many Christians have become increasingly aware of the ways in which the tongue can *"exclude,"* that is, to the ways in which the words we use can consciously or unconsciously give expression to sexism, racism, and other prejudices. Thus many Christians have committed themselves to the use of *"inclusive language,"* for it is not a trivial matter: It addresses the question of who is included in God's grace and bears as well on our imaging and understanding of God's presence in our lives. Interestingly, James is a model of disciplined, inclusive speech, for the letter balances male and female imagery in a manner quite unique in the New Testament (cf. 1:17-18; 2:15, 21-25).

In the church and in our society at large, we are also becoming increasingly conscious of the power of words to disempower and humiliate. While attention to this matter centers on appropriate speech between men and women, it also bears on the manner in which parents and children, husbands and wives, and teachers and students speak to each other. Moreover, "*gossip*" is a constant theme of community life. Thus an oft-repeated remark gives expression to what is often our community spirit: "*If you can't say something good about someone, come over here and sit next to me.*"

It is important for Christians to talk with and about each other in order that they may know and care for each other. After all, Christians are members of a family by virtue of baptism and should aspire to be the sort of people who know a great deal about one another without using that information to hurt one another. Reflection on James may help us turn our tongues to constructive rather than destructive ends.

Finally, in connection with James' discussion, it is important to remember that the tongue's potential for evil can also include silence. Sometimes failure to speak – failure to use our tongues – can damage our family, church, or community (local, national, international) relationships. Thus we should note that James does not counsel us to *"zipper"* the tongue. Instead we are urged to *"bridle"* it (1:26; 3:2). The bridle does not stop the horse from running; it helps the horse run in a more disciplined direction. This is James' hope for Christian speech.

James 3:13~18 → Two Kinds of Wisdom

NIV	TT
[13] Who is wise and understanding among you? Let them show it by their good life, by deeds done in the humility that comes from wisdom. [14] But if you harbor bitter envy and selfish ambition in your hearts, do not boast about it or deny the truth. [15] Such "wisdom" does not come down from heaven but is earthly, unspiritual, demonic. [16] For where you have envy and selfish ambition, there you find disorder and every evil practice. [17] But the wisdom that comes from heaven is first of all pure; then peace-loving, considerate, submissive, full of mercy and good fruit, impartial and sincere. [18] Peacemakers who sow in peace reap a harvest of righteousness.	[13] Who is wise and understanding among you? Show it by your good life that your works are done with gentleness born of wisdom. [14] But if you have bitter envy and selfish ambition in your hearts, do not be boastful and false to the truth. [15] Such wisdom does not come **from above**[30], but is earthly, unspiritual, devilish. [16] For where there is envy and selfish ambition, there will also be disorder and wickedness of every kind. [17] But the wisdom from above is first pure, then peaceable, gentle, willing to yield, full of mercy and good fruits, without a trace of partiality or hypocrisy. [18] And a harvest of righteousness is sown in peace for those who make peace.

---

[30] ἄνωθεν → It means *"from above," "from the beginning," "for a long time," "again,"* and *"anew."* (See Excursus 11: *"From Above"*)

Throughout the Book of James, the *"double-minded person"* has been continually before us: the person who looks both to the world and to God for values and security and so compromises his or her integrity of faith; the person prone to double-talk, double-face, double-vision. Double-mindedness may be a particular peril to Christians who live in a cultural context where it is often assumed that the values of God and the values of their society are one and the same. However, James reminds us that what God values and what the world values are quite dissimilar. t.

- **13 – 18** The challenge to fence-sitters is presented by means of two pointed contrasts. The first is a contrast between two kinds of wisdom: a true wisdom that *"comes down from above"* and a pseudo-wisdom that is *"earthly, unspiritual, devilish."* The true wisdom of which James speaks has little to do with intellectual brilliance. It is not a wisdom that is achieved by going to school. As stated in 1:5, it is entirely a gift of God, *"who gives to all generously and ungrudgingly."* This wisdom consists of knowledge of how to live according to God's ways. Thus the truly *"wise and understanding"* person manifests his or her wisdom not by superior arguments or brilliance of mind, but by a *"good life"* – by *"works"* that *"are done with gentleness born of wisdom."* Once again James declares that actions speak louder than words! True wisdom is manifested in one's conduct – in a manner of life that is, above all, peaceable.

  According to James, quarrelsome behavior belies any claim to true wisdom. True wisdom leads to peaceable conduct, not to jealousy or selfish ambition, desires which destroy the fabric of human community. Divisive behaviors are inspired by a malevolent sort of *"wisdom,"* a false wisdom that is *"earthly, unspiritual, devilish"* – that is, the sort of wisdom that a demon might possess! For just as the demon's *"faith"* (2:19) fails to manifests itself in works that are faith's proper expression, so too does earthly, unspiritual, demonic *"wisdom"* fail to manifest itself in deeds of righteousness and peacemaking.

Excursus 11: *"From Above"*

The term, *"ἄνωθεν"* which can mean *"from above"* or *"again"* appears 13 times in the New Testament. James uses this word to emphasize that *"every good and perfect gift is from above,"* especially true wisdom, coming down to us from the Father (Jas. 1:18; 3:15, 17). We can only receive wisdom as a gift from God through His Spirit (cf. 1 Cor. 2:6-16). However, the most significant use of *"ἄνωθεν"* occurs in John 3:3, 7, when Jesus tells Nicodemus that he must be *"born again"* (or does it mean *"born from above"*?). We really do not need to choose between these two options, for when we are born *"from above"* (i.e., *"born of the Spirit of God"*), we experience *"rebirth"* (i.e., *"we are born again"*). The ambiguity in the word beautifully covers both concepts.

James 4:1~6 → Friendship with the World or Friendship with God?

NIV	TT
4 ¹ What causes fights and quarrels among you? Don't they come from your desires that battle within you? ² You desire but do not have, so you kill. You covet but you cannot get what you want, so you quarrel and fight. You do not have because you do not ask God. ³ When you ask, you do not receive, because you ask with wrong motives, that you may spend what you get on your pleasures. ⁴ You adulterous people, don't you know that friendship with the world means enmity against God? Therefore, anyone who chooses to be a friend of the world becomes an	4 ¹ Those conflicts and disputes among you, where do they come from? Do they not come from your cravings that are at war within you? ² You want something and do not have it; so you commit murder. And you covet something and cannot obtain it; so you engage in disputes and conflicts. You do not have, because you do not ask. ³ You ask and do not receive, because you ask wrongly, in order to spend what you get on your pleasures. ⁴ **Adulterers!**[31] Do you not know that friendship with the world is enmity with God? Therefore whoever wishes to be a friend of the world becomes an enemy of God. ⁵ Or do you suppose that it is for nothing that the scripture

---

[31] μοιχαλίδες → It means "*adulteresses*," or "*adulterous people*." It probably recalls Israel's unfaithfulness to God. The uncompromising choice between God and the world echoes Jesus in Matt. 6:24 and even earlier, the two ways of Joshua (Josh. 24:14-15) and of Moses (Deut. 30:19).

enemy of God. ⁵ Or do you think Scripture says without reason that he jealously longs for the spirit he has caused to dwell in us? ⁶ But he gives us more grace. That is why Scripture says: "God opposes the proud, but shows favor to the humble."	says, "**God yearns jealously for the spirit that He has made to dwell in us**"?³² ⁶ But he gives all the more grace; therefore it says, "**God opposes the proud, but gives grace to the humble**."³³

The second contrast is stated even more sharply. Fence-sitters are challenged to choose between two alternatives: friendship with the world or friendship with God.

- **1 – 6** James has already suggested in 1:27 that genuine religion consists of keeping oneself *"unstained by the world."* This does not mean that Christians are to refrain from taking part in the world's affairs, as we noted earlier, but that they should not embrace the world's standards. The term world refers to ways of thinking and systems of values that do not take God's existence and God's claims into account. Christians are to be engaged in the world, but with a different understanding of reality and a different set of values,

---

³² πρὸς φθόνον ἐπιποθεῖ τὸ πνεῦμα ὃ κατῴκισεν ἐν ἡμῖν → This phrase can be translated as *"that God jealously longs for the spirit that he made to live in us"* or *"that the Spirit God caused to live in us longs jealously."* It seems and sounds like the Scripture was being quoted or paraphrased. However, there is no record of such a text, in or out of the Bible.

³³ From Prov. 3:34

informed by the experience of the grace of God in Jesus Christ.

In 4:1-4, James further unmasks the worldly disposition: It is one that places self and the pursuit of pleasure at the center of one's aspirations and activities. As a result, it tends toward a life that is largely destructive of people. Self-centered enviousness leads to covetousness, disputes, conflicts, and even murder. Moreover, it is a disposition that leads one to forego prayer, or to use prayer as one more means to gratify desires.

"Envy" and *"covetousness"* are emphasized repeatedly in 3:13-4:6 for, in James' view, they are at the heart of all human conflict and a central mark of friendship with the world and of wisdom from below. And are not envy and covetousness in fact often the enemy of personal peace, peace in the family, peace in the church, peace in the nation, and peace in the world?

James' indictment issues in a harsh rebuke: *"Adulterers!"* James draws on a familiar biblical imagery, which compares the relationship between God and the chosen people as a marriage, when he gives this rebuke to the *"unfaithful partner"*: *"Do you not know that friendship with the world is enmity with God?"* The rich imagery of a marriage gives expression to the exclusive commitment and devotion demanded of God's people.

James also draws on the language of friendship. For James, friendship has a special meaning. As I noted earlier (see page 61), friendship was not a casual affection in the first-century world. It was a much discussed and highly esteemed relationship. Indeed, friends were considered "*one soul*," which meant "*at the least, to share the same attitudes and values and perceptions, to see things the same way.*"

One must choose between friendship with the world and friendship with God, for it is not possible to share the attitudes, values, and perceptions of both God and the world simultaneously! A double-minded person wishes to be a friend of both! These two ways of life are simply incompatible; they are mutually exclusive. Indeed, James states that "*whoever wishes to be a friend of the world becomes an enemy of God.*"

Double-mindedness grieves our rejected partner and friend, as well as evokes divine jealously. God yearns for our single-minded devotion and desires for our return. James reminds us in verse 6 that we may return to God in humble repentance, and the relationship will be graciously restored.

James 4:7~12 → Call to Repentance

NIV	TT
[7] Submit yourselves, then, to God. Resist the devil, and he will flee from you. [8] Come near to God and he will come near to you. Wash your hands, you sinners, and purify your hearts, you double-minded. [9] Grieve, mourn and wail. Change your laughter to mourning and your joy to gloom. [10] Humble yourselves before the Lord, and he will lift you up.	[7] Submit yourselves therefore to God. Resist the **devil**[34], and he will flee from you. [8] Draw near to God, and he will draw near to you. Cleanse your hands, you sinners, and purify your hearts, you double-minded. [9] Lament and mourn and weep. **Turn**[35] your laughter into mourning and your joy into dejection. [10] Humble yourselves before the Lord, and he will exalt you.
[11] Brothers and sisters, do not slander one another. Anyone who speaks against a brother or sister or judges them speaks against the law and judges it. When you judge the law, you are not keeping it, but sitting in judgment on it. [12] There is only one Lawgiver and Judge, the one who is able to	[11] Do not speak evil against one another, brothers and sisters. Whoever speaks evil against another or judges another, speaks evil against the law and judges the law; but if you judge the law, you are not a doer of the law but a judge. [12] There is one lawgiver and judge who is able to save

---

[34] διάβολος → It means "*slanderer*," and "*devil*." (See Excursus 12: The Devil)

[35] μετατραπήτω → It means "*to turn around*" or "*be turned*." This term in a passive voice only appears here in the New Testament.

| save and destroy. But you— who are you to judge your neighbor? | and to destroy. So who, then, are you to judge your neighbor? |

Verses 7-10 contain ten imperatives, all of them concise, crisp, and like maxims in general, portable to a range of contexts (Submit, resist, draw near, cleanse, purify, lament, mourn, weep, turn around, and humble). Whether the writer is drawing on a collection of moral instructions is not clear, but one wonders, when one sees that the three times in 4:6-7 are found in 1 Pet. 5:5-9, and in the same order. Antecedents to all ten imperatives are found in early Judaism among those who presented Israel's faith as moral instruction rather than as ritual and historical memories. All ten imperatives in vv.7-10 deal with one's relation to God, while vv.11-12 concern one's relation to the neighbor.

Excursus 12: The Devil

James 4:7 is the only reference to the devil in the letter, though demons are mentioned in 2:19. James reflects Judaism's acknowledgement of God's sovereignty; the devil is in no sense God's equal – there is but one God (2:19). James' spiritual dualism gives the devil less due than is common in many *"Conservative" "Evangelical"* or *"Pentecostal"* circles. James lays responsibility for sin's origin squarely in the desires of human hearts (1:14-15; 4:1-3); *"the devil made me do it,"* a line popularized by Flip Wilson's character Geraldine, does not excuse. For James the *"devil"* is an opponent who will flee if met with staunch resistance (4:7; cf. Matt. 16:18). The devil is resisted by rejecting that *"devilish"* understanding (3:15) that drives those who serve self rather than serve God through demonstrations of mercy. Such faithful resistance in the struggle for God's cause is an important theme in the Book of James (e.g., 1:12; 5:11).

- **7 – 10** Two distinct ways of life, then, lie before Christians, and we are challenged to choose which one we will embrace. We can embrace *"wisdom from below"* and *"friendship with the world"* and exist as if God has no claim on our lives, if we so choose. However, God has made available another way of life. Through the gift of the gospel – the *"implanted word"* – in our lives (1:21), through the gift of God's *"wisdom from above,"* we have been empowered to embrace God's own intentions for human life.

  Having sharply stated the two incompatible options before us, James calls for a radical decision on our part. We are called away from uncommitted double-mindedness to single-minded devotion to God. We are called to terminate our affair with the world and to renew our friendship with God.

  Verses 7-10 begins and ends with the theme of humility, already frequent in the letter. Clean hands and pure hearts (v.8), while originating in the rituals of the priesthood (Exod. 30:17-21), came to be used widely in a moral sense (Psalms 24:4; 73:13; *Sir.* 38:10). Verse 9 uses the dramatic and emotional imagery of biblical Judaism to call for repentance and sorrow for sin. The exaltation of those who humble themselves echoes a teaching of Jesus (Matt. 23:12; Luke 18:14).

  These concluding verses constitute, in effect, a call to radical repentance. That call is accompanied by reassurance that God's response will be one of expansive graciousness. Right relationship to God, however, also bears on our relationship to others. Thus, in the final verses, James addresses the necessity for right relationships among fellow Christians.

- **11 – 12** Verses 11-12 set the reader, not before God, but in the presence of the brothers and sisters and neighbor. Speaking (1:19-20, 26; 3:1-12), judging (2:13), and law (1:22-25; 2:8-12) have been treated previously, but now are tightly drawn in one brief passage that concludes the discussion of conflict in the Christian community. Addressing the readers as brothers and sisters sets in sharp relief the issue of criticism and slander against one's brothers and sisters. The law against slander was clear (Lev. 19:16), just as it was on love of neighbor (Lev. 19:18). In the writer's movement of thought, to speak against a brother or sister is to "*speak against the law*" that forbids it. Just as speaking against another is judging another, speaking against the law is judging the law. Judging the law is putting oneself above the law, and to put oneself above the law is to sit in God's seat. However, we know there is only one God, one giver of law, one judge. Conclusion: do not even begin this dangerous and futile journey by slandering or speaking against a neighbor. '*Who do you think you are?*' is a sharp way to end such discussion.

Perhaps it is good to remind ourselves that the letter is addressed to people who have already heard the gospel, to people who have already been made friends of God through Jesus Christ! This passage reminds us that our friendship with God, like all friendships, is a living reality and must continually be nourished and renewed. Living the Christian life entails continual recommitment to sharing the attitudes, values, and perceptions of God – to embodying God's own intentions for human life.

James 4:13~17 → Faith and Business Practice

NIV	TT
[13] Now listen, you who say, "Today or tomorrow we will go to this or that city, spend a year there, carry on business and make money." [14] Why, you do not even know what will happen tomorrow. What is your life? You are a mist that appears for a little while and then vanishes. [15] Instead, you ought to say, "If it is the Lord's will, we will live and do this or that." [16] As it is, you boast in your arrogant schemes. All such boasting is evil. [17] If anyone, then, knows the good they ought to do and doesn't do it, it is sin for them.	[13] Come now, you who say, "Today or tomorrow we will go to such and such a town and spend a year there, doing business and making money." [14] Yet you do not even know what tomorrow will bring. What is your life? For you are a mist that appears for a little while and then vanishes. [15] Instead, you ought to say, "If the Lord wishes, we will live and do this or that." [16] As it is, you boast in your arrogance; all such boasting is evil. [17] Anyone, then, who knows the right thing to do and fails to do it, commits sin.

The Book of James insists that faith transforms routine pursuits into arenas for discipleship. Business practices are not excluded. Indeed James sharply chastises any who neglect God's sovereignty over commercial endeavors.

- **13 – 17** *"Come now, you who say, 'Today or tomorrow we will go to such and such a town and spend a year there, doing business and making money'"* (v.13). James does not chastise business practices as such. It does not condemn intelligent planning for the future.

What is rebuked is the arrogant assumption that life consists of doing business and making money, that human calculation can secure the future. James mocks any such arrogance by forcefully reminding us that all our projects – indeed our very lives – are provisional. Again the author centers on boasting and arrogance (2:13; 3:14) as the root of the problem. Life is uncertain and transitory. The future is not in our control, and we do not know what it will bring. In everything, we are utterly dependent upon the living God.

Thus, instead of assuming that we are self-sufficient or that we control our destiny, we should acknowledge our dependence upon God. We ought to say that *"If the Lord wishes, we will live and do this or that."* In fact, the familiar expression, *"God willing,"* is attributed to James. We are to commit our plans to the will of God.

Moreover, we are to apply our faith to our business practices. God is sovereign over all of life, and our business pursuits, like all the activities of our lives, are to be informed and transformed by God's presence, power, and intentions – or else we are liable to sin.

Indeed we sin not only by doing what is wrong. *"Anyone who knows the right thing to do and fails to do it, commits sin"* as well. Thus we are encouraged to embody God's intentions for human life in our business practices and in all our endeavors.

James 5:1~6 → Denunciation of the Rich

NIV	TT
5 ¹ Now listen, you rich people, weep and wail because of the misery that is coming on you. ² Your wealth has rotted, and moths have eaten your clothes. ³ Your gold and silver are corroded. Their corrosion will testify against you and eat your flesh like fire. You have hoarded wealth in the last days. ⁴ Look! The wages you failed to pay the workers who mowed your fields are crying out against you. The cries of the harvesters have reached the ears of the Lord Almighty. ⁵ You have lived on earth in luxury and self-indulgence. You have fattened yourselves in the day of slaughter. ⁶ You have condemned and murdered the innocent one, who was not opposing you.	5 ¹ Come now, you rich people, weep and wail for the miseries that are coming to you. ² Your riches have rotted, and your clothes are moth-eaten. ³ Your gold and silver have rusted, and their rust will be evidence against you, and it will eat your flesh like fire. You have laid up treasure for the last days. ⁴ Listen! The wages of the laborers who mowed your fields, which you kept back by fraud, cry out, and the cries of the harvesters have reached the ears of the **Lord Sabaoth**[36]. ⁵ You have lived on the earth in luxury and in pleasure; you have fattened your hearts in a day of slaughter. ⁶ You have condemned and murdered the righteous one, who does not resist you.

---

[36] κυρίου σαβαώθ → Literally, it means "*Lord of Sabaoth.*" "*Sabaoth*" is a Hebrew term for "*armies,*" or "*hosts,*" an image of a militant God opposing evil.

With a sudden shift to prophetic condemnation (cf. Isa. 13:6; Ezek. 7:19-20; Amos 8:3, 9), James announces the woes to come upon the rich. For them, the coming of the Lord will mean condemnation and destruction (vv. 1, 3, 5). The woe oracle seals the doom of the rich oppressors. It does not summon them to repentance. With biting sarcasm, James describes the wealth that the rich store up as both evidence and fiery torment on the day of judgment (v.3).

- **1 – 6** We have had reason to suspect that the author of James is not positively inclined toward the rich (1:9-11; 2:6-7)! But now there may be no doubt about his animosity, for he unleashes his fury in fierce denunciations. The rich are invited to *"weep and wail*

  The rich are warned of the loss of their possessions: *"Your riches have rotted, and your clothes are moth-eaten. Your gold and silver have rusted."* Moreover, *"their rust will be evidence against"* them, testifying to the fact that it has lain idle and has not been used to benefit others.

  Three specific charges are then leveled against the rich. First, James declares them guilty of oppression. They have abused their position of power as employers, exploiting the poor by withholding the wages of laborers (cf. Deut. 24:14-15). Day laborers depended completely on their meager pay. To withhold their wages was to attack their very lives, also such fraud was a violation of the law of God (Lev. 19:13; Jer. 22:13). For this reason, James strikingly depicts wages as the very blood of the workers crying out in protest against injustice and declares that these cries, along with the cries of the exploited laborers themselves, *"have reached the ears of the Lord Sabaoth."* In fact, the prophetic word against such oppression in Mal. 3:5 includes the same expression for God as here: *"the Lord of Hosts."*

Second, James censures the rich for their pampered lives: *"You have lived on the earth in luxury and in pleasure."* The hardship they have inflicted on others stands in sharp contrast to the softness of their own living. James explicitly notes that they lived *"on the earth"* in a self-indulgent manner – a state that will not last forever.

The final charge against the rich is the most serious: you have *"murdered the righteous one"* (v.6). There is no reason to take this as a reference to the death of Jesus. More likely it is a vivid statement of their crime against the passive and powerless poor: *"To take away a neighbor's living is to commit murder; to deprive an employee of wages is to shed blood"* (*Sir.* 34:26).

In other words, the harsh words of condemnation in 5:1-6 are *"good news"* to the people whom James first addressed. For what James announces is that there will come a day when the poor will be lifted up and when the rich will be held accountable for injustice. These words continue to be good news to the poor of this world to this day.

North American Christian congregations, however, are wealthy when measured by international standards. Is James' angry tirade relevant to our lives? Absolutely! It continues to serve as a warning of the dangers of riches.

Moreover, this passage reminds us that God wills justice for the poor and that God hears the cries of the oppressed. And if this is so, are we not called to redress the crippling inequities and injustices with which many of our brothers and sisters must daily contend? As James so forcefully reminds us, *"faith by itself, if it has no works, is dead"* (2:17).

James 5:7~11 → The Future Horizon

NIV	TT
[7] Be patient, then, brothers and sisters, until the Lord's coming. See how the farmer waits for the land to yield its valuable crop, patiently waiting for the autumn and spring rains. [8] You too, be patient and stand firm, because the Lord's coming is near. [9] Don't grumble against one another, brothers and sisters, or you will be judged. The Judge is standing at the door!	[7] Be patient, therefore, beloved, until the coming of the Lord. The farmer waits for the precious crop from the earth, being patient with it until it receives the early and the late rains. [8] You also most be patient. Strengthen your hearts, for the **Parousia**[37] of the Lord is near. [9] Beloved, do not grumble against one another, so that you may not be judged. See, the judge is standing at the doors! [10] As an example of suffering and patience, beloved, take the prophets who spoke in the name of the Lord. [11] Indeed we call blessed those who showed endurance. You have heard of the endurance of Job, and you have seen the purpose of the Lord, how the Lord is compassionate and merciful.
[10] Brothers and sisters, as an example of patience in the face of suffering, take the prophets who spoke in the name of the Lord. [11] As you know, we count as blessed those who have persevered. You have heard of Job's perseverance and have seen what the Lord finally brought about. The Lord is full of compassion and mercy.	

---

[37] παρουσία → It means "*coming*," "*advent*," "*presence*," and "*Parousia*." (See Excursus 13: Parousia)

One of the fastest growing religious constituencies today is that of *"believers, but not belongers"* – people who say they hold to religious beliefs but who choose not to participate in a local congregation or to identify themselves with the community of faith through the ages. But to James' way of thinking, there is no such thing as a private Christian. To be a Christian is to be part of a community of faith. Thus the closing words of the letter seek to strengthen the faithful in their common life. James' counsel is threefold: (1) The community is to wait patiently for the Parousia of the Lord (5:7-11); (2) it is to be united in prayer (5:12-18); (3) its members are to demonstrate care and concern for one another (5:19-20).

- **7 – 11** The angry threats subside, and the tone changes dramatically as James encourages the Christian community: *"Be patient, therefore, beloved, until the coming of the Lord."*

  Many of James' first readers were in much need of encouragement. Some experienced hardship at the hands of the rich (cf. 2:6-7; 5:1-6). Whatever the nature of their difficulties, or of ours, believers are encouraged to be patient in view of the imminent Parousia of the Lord. A model of fortitude is provided: the farmer who *"waits for the precious crop from the earth, being patient with it until it receives the early and the late rains."*

  In addition, James commends two examples of patience under hardship; The Old Testament prophets, whose struggles against opposition and rejection and temptations to despair (cf. Jer. 20:7-9) were well known;

and the proverbially patient Job, an example likely to surprise those who are familiar with the defiant Job of the canonical book. In chapter 3 – 31 of the Old Testament book, Job agonizes over his predicament and struggles loudly and bitterly with his pain before well-meaning friends and the Almighty. Nevertheless, he clings tenaciously to God and refuses to yield to atheism. Thus patience or *"endurance"* is not equated with passive resignation. What James recommends is active perseverance – a steadfast, heroic constancy of faith. Those who know the outcome of Job's story (*"the purpose of the Lord"* [James 5:11]; compare Job 42:12) can be confident that their hope, too, is in this *"compassionate and merciful"* God.

Excursus 13: Parousia

This "παρουσία" is a rich term. In English, translators generally translate it as *"come,"* or *"advent,"* the Church translates it as *"the second coming."* Those translations are fine. I do not have any problems with those translations. However, one thinks it is important to look at it in its context. Historically the term, "παρουσία" (Parousia) had two meanings. One the one hand the word served to describe a sacred expression, *"the coming of a hidden divinity – who makes his presence felt by a revelation of his power, or whose presence is celebrated in the cult."* On the other hand, the term became the official Roman term *"for a visit of a person of high rank,"* especially *"of kings and emperors visiting a province."*

Christians writers took these two expressions to describe *"the Second Coming of Jesus,"* or *"Parousia"* as *"Jesus' Messianic Advent in glory to judge the world*

---

at the end of the age."

To be sure, the author of James believed that Christ would return during his lifetime, as did other first-century Christians (cf. 1 Thess. 4:14-17). We no longer live with the same sense of imminent expectation. Nevertheless, hope in Christ's coming again is still an essential article of Christian faith. We are to wait patiently and to live in hope, assured that whatever difficulties beset us, the ultimate fact for the world will be the power and love of God.

God has a gracious, saving purpose for the world – a purpose seen clearly in Jesus Christ. And God will not fail to achieve that redemptive purpose in the world despite all appearances to the contrary. Christ will come again, and God's reign will be established in fullness: *"a new heaven and a new earth"* (Rev. 21:1). To that end we pray, *"Your kingdom come, your will be done on earth as it is in heaven."* Thus we too can move into the future with patient trust and confidence, knowing that the future belongs to God.

James 5:12~18 → The Importance of Prayer

NIV	TT
[12] Above all, my brothers and sisters, do not swear— not by heaven or by earth or by anything else. All you need to say is a simple "Yes" or "No." Otherwise you will be condemned. [13] Is anyone among you in trouble? Let them pray. Is anyone happy? Let them sing songs of praise. [14] Is anyone among you sick? Let them call the elders of the church to pray over them and anoint them with oil in the name of the Lord. [15] And the prayer offered in faith will make the sick person well; the Lord will raise them up. If they have sinned, they will be forgiven. [16] Therefore confess your sins to each other and pray for each other so that you may be healed. The prayer of a righteous person is	[12] Above all, my beloved, do not swear, either by heaven or by earth or by any other oath, but let your "Yes" be yes and your "No" be no, so that you may not fall under condemnation. [13] Are any among you suffering? They should pray. Are any cheerful? They should sing songs of praise. [14] Are any among you sick? They should call for the elders of the **ecclesia**[38] and have them pray over them, anointing them with oil in the name of the Lord. [15] The prayer of faith will save the sick, and the Lord will raise them up; and anyone who has committed sins will be forgiven. [16] Therefore confess your sins to one another, and pray for one another, so that you may be healed. The prayer of the righteous is powerful and effective. [17] Elijah was a

---

[38] ἐκκλησία → It means *"to call out,"* *"assembly,"* and *"church."* (see Excursus 14: Ecclesia)

powerful and effective. [17] Elijah was a human being, even as we are. He prayed earnestly that it would not rain, and it did not rain on the land for three and a half years. [18] Again he prayed, and the heavens gave rain, and the earth produced its crops.	human being like us, and he prayed fervently that it might not rain, and for three years and six months it did not rain on earth. [18] Then he prayed again, and the heaven gave rain and the earth yielded its harvest.

The Christian community is also to be united in prayer, which is a vital aspect of the community's life. Earlier, James has indicated that there are inappropriate ways of calling upon God (1:6; 4:3), and one more is noted: that of swearing *"by heaven or by earth or by any other oath."* This text addresses the appropriate forms of prayer.

- **12 – 18** James is not speaking here of profanity, or of the oaths required in legal or civil proceedings. What James condemns is the practice of appealing to God or to something sacred in order to buttress the truthfulness of a statement or promise. Swearing by oath is unnecessary for Christians, who should always be honest and sincere in relations with others. A simple yes or no should suffice (cf. Matt. 5:33-37). This letter addresses the appropriate forms of prayer.

1. We are to pray when we are suffering – that God may strengthen us, direct us, and give us assurance to press on.

2. We are to pray when we are cheerful – in thanksgiving for the grace of God, which blesses us with experiences of fullness.

3. We are to pray when we are sick – calling upon the healing power of God, who wills our restoration and wholeness.

All the circumstances of our lives are then occasions of prayer! Moreover, prayer is not only personal, it is also communal. Believers are encouraged to join the power of personal prayer with the prayer of others. The sick are instructed to *"call for the elders of the ecclesia and have them pray over them, anointing them with oil in the name of the Lord."* The *"elders,"* it seems, took special responsibility for the physical as well as spiritual good of the congregation. Thus they would gather to pray for and with the sick and to anoint them with oil. In the ancient world, oil had both a medicinal and a liturgical purpose. James makes it clear that it is not the oil but the power of God in response to faithful prayer that brings healing from sickness (5:15).

Excursus 14: Ecclesia (*"ἐκκλησίᾳ"*)

The term *"ἐκκλησίᾳ"* appear 114 times in the New Testament. It is derived from *"ἐκκλησία"* (*"to call out"*), so the church, *"assembly"* is the *"called-out ones"* of God. In its secular use *"ἐκκλησίᾳ"* refers to the gathering of the competent citizens of a city-state to order to decide issues regarding laws, office appointments, and public policy. But the prototype of the NT *"ἐκκλησίᾳ"* lies not in Greco-

---

Roman history but in the assembly of God's people in the OT (cf. Acts 7:38), which developed into the Jewish synagogue as the gathering of the community of God. But while the "ἐκκλησίᾳ" may find its roots in the synagogue, it is not a subset of it but becomes the new term used for the gathering of various groups of Christian believers.

It is noteworthy that the only occurrences of "ἐκκλησίᾳ" in the gospels are in the Gospel of Matthew (Matt. 16:18; 18:17). Jesus promises to build his church, and he instructs his followers to practice disciple in the church. Luke uses this word only in the Book of Acts. "ἐκκλησίᾳ" is basically a Pauline term (more than half of its NT uses are in his letters). Paul never thinks of the church as a physical structure but as a dedicated group of disciples of Jesus Christ (Phlm. 2; Col. 4:15), whom he has purchased with his blood (Rev. 5:9). The Apostle sees the church as a new race, which he lists it alongside Jews and Greeks in 1 Cor. 10:32; it is sufficiently equipped with leadership and gifts to fulfill God's purposes on earth (1 Cor. 12:28); and it is the avenue through which "*the Wisdom of God*" is made known (Eph. 1:22).

James also affirms that if the sick person has committed a sin (an ancient view), he or she will be forgiven. A direct connection between sickness and sin is not necessarily assumed, but a possible connection may be implied. Whatever one may think of this ancient view, Christians today affirm that God wills restoration to both physical and spiritual wholeness.

This latter aspect of human wholeness is directly addressed in 5:16. James acknowledges the reality of sin. It remains a fact of Christian life. The proper response to it is prayer. Believers are encouraged to confess their sins to one another and to pray for one another, so that they may be restored to wholeness of life. The prayer of all believing petitioners is powerful and effective. Great results can be expected through prayer.

Lest there be any doubt about this, James points to the prophet Elijah to demonstrate how effective and powerful prayer can be. James emphasizes Elijah's energy in prayer (*"he prayed fervently"*) and his humanity. The one who prayed with such great effect was an ordinary *"human being like us."* In other words, our prayers can be no less effective. James encourages Christians to place great confidence in prayer. (See Excursus 15: Confidence in Prayer)

Excursus 15: Confidence in Prayer

Some sayings of Jesus could (and have) given rise to mistaken beliefs that prayer is a "blank check" and God is some kind of shopping network.

"Whatever you ask for in prayer with faith, you will receive." (Matt. 21:22)
"Ask, and it will be given you; search, and you will find; knock, and the door will be opened for you." (Matt. 7:7)
"If you then, who are evil, know how to give good gifts to your children, how much more will your Father in heaven give good things to those who ask him!" (Matt. 7:11)
"Ask whatever you wish, and it will be given you." (John 15:7b)

James juxtaposes faith in prayer with the rality that

---

those who stand firm for God's cause often suffer in the struggle. Faith does not inoculate believers from trouble.

James 5:19~20 → Care and Concern for One Another

NIV	TT
[19] My brothers and sisters, if one of you should wander from the truth and someone should bring that person back, [20] remember this: Whoever turns a sinner from the error of their way will save them from death and cover over a multitude of sins.	[19] My brothers and sisters, if anyone among you wanders from the **truth**[39] and is brought back by another, [20] you should know that whoever brings back a sinner from wandering will save the sinner's soul from death and will cover a multitude of sins.

In closing, James encourages members of the Christian community to have greater care and concern for one another. Sin is a fact of life, and Christians do wander away at times "*from the truth*" and from the community. James focuses not on the person who sins, but on the responsibility incumbent upon other Christians to seek actively to restore the sinner.

- **19 – 20** Matthew's treatment of the parable of the lost sheep (Matt. 18:10-14) highlights the responsibility of community leaders to seek out Christians who have gone astray. Christians are not to give up on each other! We have a responsibility for brothers and sisters in Christ who wander from our fellowship. We are to

---

[39] ἀλήθεια →It means "*truth*," "*uprightness*," "*reality*," and "*dependability*." The use of "the truth" in 3:14 implies moral rather than doctrinal content, and that may be the sense here.

seek to win them back and preserve them from error. When confronted with human sin, our attitude is always to be one of restoration rather than condemnation. James concludes with a partial citation of Prov. 10:12b. The Proverbs text speaks of love covering a multitude of sins. If James had the full citation in mind, then the rescue of the sinner might be an example of the love that fulfills the *"royal law"* (2:8). The conclusion encourages readers to recognize that *"mercy triumphs over judgment"* (2:13b). The perfect wisdom that James encourages Christians to seek from God does not mean perfectionism. Though members of the Christian community should seek out wisdom, single-minded obedience to God, and love of others, failure to achieve that goal should not cause discouragement. The *"synagogue,"* *"ecclesia,"* Church that heeds the exhortations in the Book of James, *"Iakwbou"* can find its way to God while it continues to live in the Diaspora.

Bibliography

Adamson, J. B. *The Epistle of James*. NICNT. Grand
   Rapids: Eerdmans, 1976.

Boring, M. Eugene, Fred B. Craddock. *The People's New
   Testament Commentary*. Louisville,KY:
   Westminster John Knox Press, 2009.

Bruce, F.F. *Zondervan Bible Commentary: One-Volume
   Illustrated Edition*. Grand Rapids, MI: Zondervan,
   2008.

Buechner, Frederick. *Telling the Truth: The Gospels as
   Tragedy, Comedy, and Fairy Tale*. Sanfrancisco:
   HarperSanFransisco, 1977.

Byron, Gay L. "James" in *True to Our Native Land*.
   Minneapolis, MN: Fortress Press, 2007.

Carson, D.A, R.T. France, J.A. Motyer, and G.J. Wenham.
   New Bible Commentary: 21st century edition.
   Nottingham, England: Inter-Varsity Press, 1994.

Charlesworth, J. H. *The Old Testament Pseudepigrapha*.
   New York, NY: Doubleday, 1985.

Church, Christopher. *Hebrews-James*, Smyth & Helwys
   Bible Commentary. Macon, Georgia: Smyth &
   Helwys Publishing, Inc. 2004.

Danker, Frederick William. *A Greek-English Lexicon of the New Testament and other Early Christian Literature Thrid Edition (BDAG)*. Chicago, IL: The University of Chicago Press, 2000.

Davids, P. H. *Commentary on James*. NIGTC. Grand Rapids: Eerdmans, 1982.

Dockery, David S. *Concise Bible Commentary*. Nashville, TN: B&H Publishing Group, 2010.

Eum, Terry Kwanghyun. *Kata Markon*. North Charleston, SC: CreateSpace, 2015.

Eum, Terry Kwanghyun. *Pros Philemona*. North Charleston, SC: CreateSpace, 2015.

Gench, Frances Taylor. *Hebrews and James*. Westminster Bible Companion. Louisville, KY: Westminster John Knox Press, 1996.

Henry, Matthew. *Zondervan NIV Matthew Henry Commentary*. Grand Rapids, MI: Zondervan. 1992.

Holladay, Carl R. *A Critical Introduction to the New Testament*. Nashville, TN: Abingdon Press, 2005.

Houston, J. M. *An Environmental Backgrounds to the New Testament*. Grand Rapids, MI: Zondervan, 1979.

Johnson, Luke T. "Friendship with the World/Friendship with God: A study of Discipleship in James," in *Discipleship in the New Testament*, ed. F. f. Segovia. Philadelphia: Fortress Press, 1985.

Johnson, Luke T. "James," in *The New Interpreter's Bible volume XII*. Nashville, TN: Abingdon Press. 1998.

King, Martin Luther, Jr. *Stride Toward Freedom: The Montgomery Story*. New York, NY: Harper & Brothers, 1958.

Mounce, William D. *Mounce's Complete Expository Dictionary of Old & New Testament Words*. Grand Rapids, MI: Zondervan. 2006.

Perkins, Pheme. *First and Second Peter, James, and Jude*. Interpretation: A Bible Commentary for Teaching and Preaching. Louisville, KY: John Knox Press, 1995.

Ward, R. B. "The Communal Concern of the Epistle of James." Ph. D. diss., Harvard University, 1966.

Wood, D. R. W. *New Bible Dictionary*. Nottingham, England: Inter-Varsity Press, 1996.

Index of Ancient and Biblical References

Index of Ancient and Biblical References

Index of Ancient and Biblical References

Made in the USA
Middletown, DE
22 September 2021